NATIVE TREES of CONNECTICUT

A Step-By-Step Illustrated Guide to
Identifying the State's Species

John Ehrenreich

Globe
Pequot

Guilford, Connecticut

Globe Pequot

An imprint of Globe Pequot, the trade division of The Rowman & Littlefield Publishing Group, Inc.
4501 Forbes Blvd., Ste. 200
Lanham, MD 20706
www.rowman.com

Distributed by NATIONAL BOOK NETWORK

British Library Cataloguing in Publication Information available

Library of Congress Cataloging-in-Publication Data
Names: Ehrenreich, John, 1943- author.
Title: Native trees of Connecticut : a step-by-step illustrated guide to
   identifying the state's species / John Ehrenreich.
Description: Guilford, Connecticut : Globe Pequot, [2022] | Includes
   bibliographical references and index. | Summary: "A step-by-step,
   illustrated guide to identifying Connecticut's trees, providing easily
   observable characteristics that can help to recognize a general type, as
   well as a distinct species identification"— Provided by publisher.
Identifiers: LCCN 2021043383 (print) | LCCN 2021043384 (ebook) | ISBN
   9781493060207 (trade paperback) | ISBN 9781493060214 (epub)
Subjects: LCSH: Trees—Connecticut—Identification. | Forest
   plants—Connecticut—Identification.
Classification: LCC QK151 .E37 2022 (print) | LCC QK151 (ebook) | DDC
   582.1609746—dc23
LC record available at https://lccn.loc.gov/2021043383
LC ebook record available at https://lccn.loc.gov/2021043384

♾️™ The paper used in this publication meets the minimum requirements of American National Standard for Information Sciences—Permanence of Paper for Printed Library Materials, ANSI/NISO Z39.48-1992.

For Sharon, the roots and trunk and branches and leaves of my life.
And for Rosa, Ben, Alex, Anna, Clara, and Baby Nu.

"If you have a sapling in your hand, and someone should say to you that the Messiah has come, stay and complete the planting, and then go to greet the Messiah."

Talmud (Avot de Rabbi Nathan, 31b)

"Even if I knew that tomorrow the world would go to pieces, I would still plant my apple tree."

Martin Luther

"What was the wood, what the tree out of which heaven and earth were fashioned?"

Rig Veda 10.31.7

"The tree which moves some to tears of joy is in the eyes of others only a green thing that stands in the way . . . As man is, so he sees."

William Blake

"If you've looked at a hundred thousand acres or so of trees — you know, a tree is a tree, how many more do you need to look at?"

Ronald Reagan

"A culture is no better than its woods."

WH Auden

CONTENTS

ACKNOWLEDGMENTS

My special thanks to Jim Cortina and Diane Nizlek, my companions on many treks through the woods. Lincoln Taiz, Professor Emeritus of Biology at University of California, Santa Cruz and a good friend since high school, provided me with a wealth of insights into the biology of trees. Thanks, too, to Jim Arigoni, Alison Brion, Miley Bull, Cathy Hagadorn, Nancy Slowik, Michelle Sikorski, and Deirdra Wallin, who shared their knowledge of trees and their never-ending enthusiasm about the natural world.

INTRODUCTION

WHY TREES MATTER

"Early settlers found nearly all of Connecticut covered by forests with open, parklike conditions. . . . Clearing land for agriculture began slowly as colonists built small subsistence farms. But by the early 1800s, the establishment of farms spread rapidly as Connecticut's farmers began to supply food and wool to a rapidly growing nation. By 1820, only 25 percent of Connecticut was forested. . . . In 1830, the Erie Canal opened and Connecticut's agricultural zenith passed. Within two decades, the small, stony farms of Connecticut were unable to compete with the larger, more mechanized farms of western New York and the Ohio River Valley. Much of the farmland became exhausted and unsuitable for continuous agricultural crops and soon was abandoned. . . . Before long, forests began to return to much of Connecticut. . . . [Today] about 60 percent of Connecticut is forested—that's 6 out of every 10 acres. . . ."

(Source: The Forests of Connecticut by Eric H. Wharton, Richard H. Widmann, Carol L. Alerich, Charles J. Barnett, Andrew J. Lister, Tonya W. Lister, Don Smith, Fred Borman; published by the USDA (United States Department of Agriculture) Forest Service; Northeastern Research Station; Resource Bulletin NE-160.)

It's easy to take trees for granted—there are so many of them! But trees play a central and sometimes unappreciated ecological role on our planet. Trees are "a simple machine needing no fuel and little maintenance, one that sequesters carbon, enriches the soil, cools the ground, scrubs the air, and scales easily to any size. A tech that copies itself and even drops food for free. A device so beautiful it's the stuff of poems." (Richard Power, *The Overstory*).

A tree's roots take up water and carry it up the tree. The water then evaporates into the atmosphere through *stomata* (tiny pores), in a process called "transpiration." A large oak tree can transpire about 40,000 gallons of water a year. This explains the use of trees such as cottonwoods and willows to drain wetlands. About 10 percent of the moisture in the atmosphere is released by trees and other plants through transpiration. The large amount of water released over a forest canopy can markedly increase water vapor in the atmosphere, increasing precipitation and cloud cover. Clear cutting has reduced the water vapor in the atmosphere over the Amazon and contributed to droughts in some of the wettest areas of the world.

Trees provide oxygen. The amount of oxygen produced by an acre of trees per year equals the amount consumed by 18 people annually. One tree produces nearly 260 pounds of oxygen each year.

Trees take up carbon dioxide. One acre of trees removes up to 2.6 tons of carbon dioxide each year. US forests offset approximately 10 to 20 percent of US emissions each year. This is one of the most important factors counteracting global warming; conversely, cutting of trees worsens global warming.

Trees hold soil in place (e.g., on riverbanks and hillsides).

Trees moderate the effects of wind, sun, rain, and temperature. Wooded areas are a bit cooler than cleared areas in summer, a bit warmer in winter.

Trees provide shelter for many kinds of animals:
- Birds build nests in the branches of many trees.
- Birds and small mammals (e.g., squirrels) nest in cavities in trees. Species especially likely to form cavities include Ash, Beech, Basswood, Cottonwood, Red Oak, and Sycamore.
- Bats, tree frogs, insects, and some small birds (e.g., Brown Creepers) nest under the shaggy bark of trees such as Shagbark Hickory.
- Beavers use trees to build their dams and their underwater lodges in the ponds created by the dams.
- Trees provide cover for owls and other birds. In winter especially, conifers (evergreen trees) and oaks, beeches, hophornbeams and other deciduous trees that retain their dead leaves into winter are especially important as sources of cover.

Trees provide food for many kinds of animals:
- Leaves (deer)
- Flowers (birds, bats, insects)
- Fruits and seeds: Acorns and hickory nuts are a preferred food source for wild turkeys, deer, and bear. Berries and seeds are an important food for birds, insects, and mammals, small and large. Humans feast on a wide variety of fruits and nuts.

- Bark (squirrels, voles, porcupines, deer)
- Shoots and twigs (deer, bears, porcupines, beaver, mice, squirrels, rabbits).
- Sap (insects, birds [sapsuckers], humans. [Think maple syrup]).
- Leaf litter (earthworms)

WHY ANOTHER TREE BOOK?

There are over 800 species of tree native to or commonly cultivated in the United States. Only about 75 of the native tree species can be found in Connecticut. By focusing on these 75, this guide eliminates more than 90 percent of the wrong identifications you can make! Because this book focuses on a limited number of trees, it can also use an especially efficient approach to identifying trees. (See "How to Use this Guide," p. 4).

The book includes only trees native to Connecticut. The idea that some plants are "native" and others are not is somewhat problematic. Although the term "native" is widely used, there is no real consensus as to what it means. One definition is that the plant grows naturally in an area, without having been introduced to the area by humans. Some botanists argue that unless a plant was present in the Americas before Columbus's voyage, it is not "native." Another, less restrictive, definition is that a native plant is one that occurs naturally in the location in which it is growing, as opposed to growing in that location only because of human actions, intentional or inadvertent.

But definitions that exclude human actions assume that humans are not part of the natural world. There is no essential difference between a seed that is transported from one place to another by a human and a seed that is transported from one place to another by a bird or by the wind. Definitions based on the time a plant appeared in a specific place are essentially arbitrary. And definitions that emphasize location as the key must deal with the fact that the range of a given plant changes over time as the result of purely "natural" (i.e., non-human) causes, such as wind, animal movement, and climate change.

I will use what seems to me a useful and more common-sense definition: If a species of tree has been present in Connecticut or neighboring states for a sustained period (say a century or more) and if it has "naturalized" (i.e., it reproduces successfully and readily on its own, without human intervention), then I will consider it as native. Thus, I include trees such as Ailanthus, White Willow, and Norway Maple that, strictly speaking, are immigrants from abroad but have effectively become native, and trees such as Black Locust that have migrated northward from the American South. Conversely, I have excluded trees such as Blue Spruce, whose presence remains largely due to intentional planting, and cultivars of non-native species (e.g., copper birch, a cultivar of the European Beech), that have been produced by selective breeding for ornamental use.

In addition to the trees described in this guide, there are several dozen species of Connecticut-native plants that usually grow as shrubs but occasionally take on a more treelike form. The classic "tree" of a child's drawing has a single trunk and a crown of foliage, while a "shrub" has multiple small branches arising from the ground. (David Sibley has suggested the following rule: "If you can walk under it, it's a tree; if you have to walk around it, it's a shrub"). But the division is somewhat arbitrary. Black Willow, Box Elder, and White Birch, among others, all usually thought of as "trees," frequently have multiple trunks, and many species of tree, if grown under harsh conditions, may remain small and shrublike. Conversely, shrubs such as Bear Oak, Winterberry, Nannyberry, and the many varieties of Hawthorn, occasionally grow into small trees, 20 or 30 feet tall. In this guide, I have included species that grow to be over 25 feet tall at least somewhat commonly and have excluded the others.

HOW TO USE THIS GUIDE

Part I: How to Identify a Tree (p. 7) helps you narrow down the identity of trees through the use of "field marks"—distinctive, easily observable characteristics such as leaves, bark, flowers, and fruits. But a caution: Trees of the same species can vary from tree to tree, and some characteristics are shared by many species.

Field mark-based identifications are intended only as a *starting point*. In some cases, a single field mark will enable you to immediately identify the particular *species* (e.g., the bark of American Beech, the leaves of Tuliptrees). In other cases, the field marks will place the tree in a particular *genus* (a group of closely related species, e.g., the Maples are all members of the genus *Acer*) or will suggest that the tree is one of several species that share that field mark. You will need to go to the more detailed descriptions in Part II to confirm your identification or to determine the species more precisely.

Beware: Nature loves to fool us. This book describes *typical* characteristics of each tree species, but there are significant variations from one tree to another tree of the same species. Even on a single tree, leaves and bark may vary (e.g., leaves at the top of the tree are directly exposed to sun and may differ from those at bottom which are more shaded; and bark on the sunny side of the tree may differ from bark on the shady side). And trees may hybridize, giving rise to offspring that show features intermediate between either of the parents.

In any case, there is no such thing as a "perfect" picture of the leaves and bark characteristic of a particular tree. Leaves in nature, as opposed to the idealized photos or drawings found in most tree guides, have tears, bites taken by insects, dried areas, areas discolored by the presence of microorganisms, or other imperfections. The leaves may differ somewhat from one tree to another of the same species and may vary even on a single tree. The bark also varies from one tree to another, and the bark of younger trees and older trees are often quite different. The photos in this book, taken in the field, reflect all of these variations and imperfections. They are *examples* of the characteristics of the leaves, bark, and other features of that species, as "typical" as any other single portrayal but certainly not universal.

Part II: The Native Trees of Connecticut (p. 59) describes each of the tree species that are native to Connecticut. For each species it describes the overall shape and form of the tree when grown in an open area, the distinctive characteristics of the bark and leaves, the habitat in which the tree is typically found, and its significance for wild birds and animals. Where it is useful for identification, the flowers, buds, fruits, and other characteristics, are also described, along with a guide to distinguishing among species that are easily confused (e.g., among sugar maples, red maples, black maples, Norway maples, and striped maples).

Part III: Frequently Asked Questions (p. 159) provides supplementary information about leaves, bark, and twigs, buds, flowers, and fruits; and a very crude guide to estimating the age of a tree.

Part I: How to Identify a Tree

WHAT TO LOOK FOR

If you are trying to identify an unfamiliar tree, carefully observe the following:

Habitat: Where does the tree grow? On a sunny upland slope? In a moist forest? On the edge of a stream or pond? In a wetland?

Overall form: How big is the tree? What shape is the tree? If the tree is in the open and not in the middle of the woods, does it look like a child's "lollipop" drawing of a tree, or is the crown more irregular? Do the branches begin low on the trunk or start only higher up? Are the main branches horizontal to the trunk or set at an angle? Do the ends of the branches swoop up or droop? Are the leaves spread more-or-less evenly or bunched up? Note that trees of various species that have grown in the open often have a distinctive shape and form, while most trees growing in the woods tend to have relatively tall, unbranched trunks with a relatively narrow crown high up.

Leaves: Do pairs of leaves originate *opposite* one another *at a single point* on a branchlet, or do they arise at different points along the branchlet, *alternating* the side of the branch they stem from? Are they *lobed* (i.e., are there deep indentations in the edges of the leaf, separating it into large subdivisions—the "lobes") or are they *unlobed*? Are they *simple* (i.e., each leaf attaches directly to the twig) or *compound* (i.e., the leaf is divided into several leaflets, either all coming off a common stem or all originating at a single point)? What shape are the leaves? How big are they? Are the edges smooth or toothed? What color are they, on the top and on the underside? Are they smooth on their underside or is the under surface covered with fine hairs? Note that the leaves may not be close to the ground; binoculars may useful.

Bark: What color is the bark? Is it smooth or rough? How deep are the furrows? Are the ridges flat on top? Are the ridges and furrows irregular or do they form a more-or-less clear pattern?

Note *other characteristics*, such as the shape and color and size of the buds at the end of the branchlets and whether the buds are smooth or covered with fine hairs; the color and texture of the small *twigs;* the presence and form of *flowers* in spring and of *seeds and fruits* in late summer and fall; *thorns* on the twigs; and any *"odd" characteristics* such as dead leaves remaining on the tree in winter.

A reproducible "Field Checklist" for recording information about a particular tree can be found on p. 57.

THE FIRST STEP:
IS IT A CONIFER OR A BROADLEAF TREE?

The first step in identifying a tree is to decide whether it is a conifer (tree with needles and cones) or a flowering (broadleaf) tree.

With a few exceptions not native to Connecticut, trees belong to one of two groups, "conifers" and "flowering" (or "broadleaf") trees. *Conifers* (botanists call them "gymnosperms") have unenclosed or "naked" seeds that appear on the surface of scales or leaves—a "cone," hence "*coni*fers." (In a few cases, such as Eastern Red Cedar and Yew, the "cones" look more like berries, but even in these cases, close examination shows a structure analogous to the classic "cone"). Most conifers have needlelike leaves. Eastern Red Cedar and Northern and Atlantic White Cedar have long, thin needle*like* leaves consisting of tightly overlapping scales.

By contrast, the "flowering" or "broadleaf" trees (botanists call flowering plants "*angiosperms*"), such as maples, hickories, and black cherries, produce seeds that are enclosed in a fruit or a pod or a shell derived from the flower. These trees have broader leaves and are often called *broadleaf* trees.

Most conifers lose only a small fraction of their leaves each fall, so they appear to be "evergreen." (American Larch is an exception; though a conifer, it sheds all its leaves each winter). By contrast, broadleaf trees lose all their leaves in winter. They are "deciduous" trees, although in some cases the dead leaves remain on the tree well into winter. (American Holly is an exception; though a broadleaf tree, it remains green year-round).

IF THE TREE IS A CONIFER:
USING NEEDLES AS FIELD MARKS

Conifers native to Connecticut include Pines, Firs, Spruces, Cedars, Yews, Larch, and Hemlock. The leaves (needles) are usually enough for identification, though there are other clues, as well.

If the tree has long, thin needles, with two, three, or five needles attached to a common point of origin on a twig, it is a **Pine** (p. 60).

If the tree has shorter needles attached on all sides of a twig, it is a **Fir** (p. 65) or a **Spruce** (p. 67).

- **Firs** have relatively soft, flattened needles and cones that are erect. The cones are rarely found on the ground.
- **Spruces** have stiff, prickly needles, square in cross-section, and cones that hang down. The cones are often found on the ground.

Other common conifers include cedars and junipers (p. 78). If the needles are made up of tightly overlapping, tiny scales in (often flattened) fan-shaped arrays, it is a **Cedar** (p. 73).

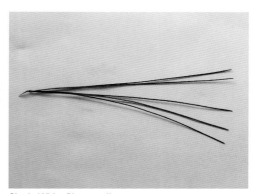

White Pine needle cluster   Single White Pine needle

Fir needles

Spruce needles

Red Cedar needles

White Cedar needles

Hemlock needles

Larch needles

If the needles are flat, less than an inch long, and appear to emerge from opposite sides of the twig, giving the sprays of needles a somewhat flattened appearance, it is a **Hemlock** (p. 76).

If the needles are more than an inch long and grow in tufts of 10-25 at the end of the twigs and along twigs, it is a **Larch** (p. 77).

IF IT IS A BROADLEAF TREE: USING LEAVES AS FIELD MARKS

What to look for

If the tree is not a conifer, the starting point for identifying the tree is usually the leaves. Look for:

- The *arrangement* of the leaves and small twigs (*opposite* or *alternating*).
- Whether the leaves are *simple* (each individual leaf is attached to the twigs by a stem or "petiole") or *compound* (made up of several leaflets coming off a common axis or originating at a single, common point)?
- Whether the leaves are *lobed* (partitioned into several sections by deep indentations) or *unlobed*.

Other characteristics:

- The *shape* of the leaves.
- The *edges* of the leaves. (Are they smooth or toothed?)
- The *thickness* of the leaves.
- The *color* of both the upper side and underside of the leaf.
- The presence or absence of fine *hairs* on the leaf's upper surface or underside or along the veins.
- Any other notable characteristics of the leaves.

Each of these leaf characteristics is discussed at greater length below.

Reminder: Leaves on different trees of the same species or even leaves on different parts of the same tree may vary. Look at several leaves to get a sense of what is "typical."

How are the twigs and leaves arranged?

In some trees, the leaves and twigs are arranged in pairs, one *opposite* the other. In other trees, the leaves are staggered along the twig and the twigs are staggered along the larger branches, *alternating* from one side to the other.

A few species have leaves arranged in whorls—three or more leaves originating from a single "node."

If it is winter and there are no leaves on the trees, look at the twigs. You can also look at the leaf scars—the marks left on twigs by the leaves after they fall off the tree—to determine whether the leaves were arranged in oppositely or alternately. Note that any given tree may have a mix of alternate and opposite leaves or branches, and that some twigs may have broken off. Look for the *preponderant* pattern.

alternate leaves

opposite leaves

alternate twigs

opposite twigs

whorled leaves

leaf scars

If a tree has oppositely arranged leaves and twigs, it is probably either a **Maple** (p. 114), an **Ash** (p. 81) a **Dogwood** (p. 100), or a **Horse Chestnut** (p. 112) (A mnemonic is "**MAD Horse**"). **Catalpa** (p. 96) sometimes has whorled leaves, sometimes opposite pairs. A few of the shrubs that occasionally take the form of a small tree (e.g., **Eastern Wahoo**, p. 152, and **Nannyberry**, p. 125, along with shrubs such as viburnum, honeysuckle, weigela, abelia, and snowberry, also have oppositely arranged leaves).

Distinguishing Among Trees with Oppositely Arranged Leaves	
Leaves are pinnately compound	Ashes
Leaves are palmately compound	Horse Chestnut
Leaves are simple, unlobed; bark is made up of small, regularly arranged, square plates	Dogwood
Leaves are simple, lobed	Maples
Large, simple leaves with rounded or heart-shaped base; some leaves in whorls rather than opposite	Catalpa
Usually a shrub. Twigs may be slightly winged. Bark of trees is distinctively furrowed.	Eastern Wahoo
Usually a shrub. Bark of trees is dark , broken into small plates.	Nannyberry

If the leaves are opposite and lobed (i.e., there are deep indentations in the edges of the leaf, separating it into subdivisions or "lobes"), it is a **Maple** (p. 114).

If the leaves are opposite but not lobed and are *"pinnately"* compound (i.e., made up of leaflets arranged on the opposite sides of a single stem) it is an **Ash** (p.

Sugar Maple leaves

Red Maple leaves

White Ash leaves

Horse Chestnut leaf

Dogwood bark

Dogwood leaves

81) The bark of mature ash trees has ridges forming a diamond-shaped pattern on the lower trunk.

If it is a small, understory tree with oval or roundish unlobed leaves and bark that forms small, regularly arranged square plates, it is a **Dogwood** (p. 100).

If the leaves are *"palmately" compound* (i.e., made up of leaflets that radiate from a single point; see below), it is a **Horse Chestnut** (p. 112).

Are the leaves simple or compound?

A *simple* leaf attaches directly to the twig and is undivided. A *compound leaf* is divided into several leaflets coming off a common axis (stem) or all originating at a single point. Sometimes it may be difficult to decide which it is. Look at the lateral buds, found at the base of the leaf, where the leaf petiole (stem) meets the branch. A simple leaf will have a bud at the base of each leaf. A compound leaf will have a bud at the base of each overall leaf but not at the base of each leaflet.

simple leaves

Trees with compound leaves

There are only a few species of tree native to Connecticut that have compound leaves. They are usually easily distinguishable one from another by their leaves and bark. Note whether the leaves are arranged in opposite or alternate or whorled fashion, whether the leaves are pinnately compound or palmately compound, and how many leaflets make up each leaf. (The number of leaflets per leaf may vary from one leaf to the next; note the range and the average number).

Pinnately compound leaves

Palmately compound leaves

Trees with compound leaves	
Palmately compound, oppositely arranged	Horse Chestnut
Pinnately compound; oppositely arranged, 5–11 leaflets	Ashes
Pinnately compound; oppositely arranged; 3–5 leaflets (may resemble poison ivy, but a tree, not a vine)	Boxelder
Pinnately compound; alternately arranged; 5–9 toothed leaflets, with the top leaflet or pairs larger than those near base	Hickories
Pinnately compound; alternately arranged; 8–23 longish leaflets attached to midrib with no stems; axis of leaves is sticky.	Butternut
Pinnately compound; alternately arranged; 8–23 leaflets with end leaflets usually smaller than others; rugged bark; axis of leaves is not sticky	Black Walnut
Pinnately compound; alternately arranged; very large leaves with up to 41 leaflets	Ailanthus
Pinnately compound; alternately arranged; 7–25 oval leaflets (not pointed at end); very rugged bark with intertwined, ropelike ridges	Black Locust
Pinnately compound; alternately arranged. Usually a shrub. Leaves have reddish petioles (stems).	Mountain Ash
Pinnately compound; alternately arranged. Usually a shrub	Sumac

A mnemonic for those with pinnately compound leaves is **LAWS? BAH!** (Black Locust, White Ash, Black Walnut, Sumac, Butternut, Ailanthus, Hickory).

If the leaves are *palmately* compound, it is a **Horse Chestnut** (p. 112).

All of the other Connecticut native trees with compound leaves are *pinnately* compound.

- If the leaves are *pinnately* compound, *very large* (up to 30" long), made up of up to 41 leaflets, and *alternately* arranged, it is an **Ailanthus** (p. 80). Each leaflet is 1"–5" long, with a few teeth near the base of the leaflet.

Ailanthus

- If the leaves are *pinnately* compound, with 5–11 leaflets shaped like long ovals with a point at the end, and *oppositely* arranged, it is an **Ash**

Ash

(p. 81). The furrows in the bark often form a distinct diamond-shaped pattern.

- If the leaves are *pinnately* compound with 3–5 leaflets and *oppositely* arranged, it is a **Boxelder** (p. 115). The leaves may look like poison ivy leaves, but Boxelder is a tree, not a vine. The leaflet shape is variable— from oval with a pointed tip to shallowly or deeply lobed. Leaf edges are smooth or have a few coarse teeth.

Boxelder

Butternut

Black Walnut

- If the leaves are *pinnately* compound, 16"–24" long with 8–23 leaflets, and *alternately* arranged, it is a **Butternut** (p. 95) or a **Black Walnut** (p. 152). Butternut and Black Walnut are very similar. The leaflets are each 2"–4.5" long, elongated ovate to broadly lance-shaped, pointed at the tip, finely toothed, and unevenly rounded at the base. The terminal leaflet may be missing. The twigs of Butternut are covered with sticky hairs, unlike Black Walnut. The underside of Butternut leaflets is densely covered with hairs, which are inconspicuous in Black Walnut.

Hickories

- If the leaves are *pinnately* compound, made up of 5–9 (sometimes more) ovate leaflets, *alternately* arranged, it is a **Hickory** (p. 105). Leaflets are typically 3"–6" long and toothed, and the terminal leaflet (or the top three leaflets) may be conspicuously larger than the leaflets lower down on the stalk.
- If the leaves are *pinnately* compound, 8"–12" long, and made up of 7–25 *smooth-edged, oval* leaflets, *alternately* arranged, it is a **Black Locust** (p. 112). Each leaflet is about 1.5" long and usually has a small point at end. The twigs usually have a pair of small thorns or spines at the base of the leaf. The bark is very rugged.

Black Locust

- If the tree is small, with multiple trunks, or even a shrub, and the leaves are *pinnately* compound, 6"–10" long, with a reddish stem and 9–17 elongated, toothed leaflets, *alternately* arranged, it is a **Mountain Ash** (p. 81). The leaflets are each 2"–4" long. In early summer, the tree

Mountain Ash

has showy white clusters of flowers, and in late summer or early fall, clusters of small (¼"–½") red or orange-red berries.

- If the tree is small or even a shrub, and the leaves are *pinnately* compound, 12"–24" long, each with 11–31 narrow, pointed leaflets, *alternately* arranged, it is one of the several species of **Sumac** (p. 148). Leaflets are 1.5"–4" long. In fall, look for large (6" long) clusters of small reddish or dark red berries at the branch tips. The fruits persist into winter.

Sumac

Trees with simple leaves

Simple leaves can be divided into those that are *lobed* (partitioned into several large sections, with rounded tips or points that stick out from the central section and deep "sinuses" or indentations) and those that are *unlobed.*

lobed leaves

unlobed leaves

Trees with simple lobed leaves

Three Connecticut-native species of tree (**Sycamore, Sassafras, Tuliptree**) and two *genuses*, each containing several species of tree (**Maples** and **Oaks**), have lobed leaves.

Trees with simple lobed leaves	
Leaves are large; the width is about the same as the length; mottled bark	Sycamore
3–5 lobes, the width is about the same or slightly wider than the length	Maples
The length of leaf greater than the width	Oaks
Four lobes, squarish, shallowly notched at top, shaped vaguely like a tulip	Tuliptree
Some leaves are three-lobed, some on the same tree are two-lobed, some on the same tree are unlobed	Sassafras

Sycamore leaf   Sycamore bark

- If the tree has *large* leaves, the width of the leaf is about the same as or a little greater than the height and the bark has peeled away in many areas (especially on the upper trunk and limbs), leaving the tree with a "camouflaged" look, it is a **Sycamore** (p. 149)
- If the width of the leaf is about the same as or slightly wider than the height (i.e., the leaf could fit inside a more-or-less *square* box) and the bark is *not* mottled, it is a **Maple** (p. 114)
- If the height of the leaf is significantly greater than the width (i.e., the

Sugar Maple leaf   Red Oak leaf

leaf could fit inside a *rectangular* box but not a square one), it is an **Oak** (p. 126).

If the tips of each lobe are pointed, the tree is in the **Red Oak** family (p. 134). If the ends are rounded, it is in the **White Oak** family (p. 142).

Red Oak   White Oak

- If the leaves are *lobed*, are generally wider at the bottom than at the top, and the tip of the lobe away from the stem is flat or shallowly notched, it is a **Tuliptree** (p. 150)
- If some of the leaves have *two lobes* (shaped like a mitten), others on the same tree *three lobes*, and still others on the same tree are *unlobed*, it is a **Sassafras** (p. 146)

Tuliptree leaf   Sassafras leaves

Identifying trees with simple, alternately arranged, unlobed leaves

The most difficult trees to identify solely by their leaves are those with *simple, alternately* arranged, *unlobed* leaves.

Start out by looking at the *shape* of the leaves (p. 26) and at their *edges* (p. 26–27). Note that the leaves on a single tree may vary somewhat (e.g., some may be roundish, others more elongated).

Then look at the *edges* of the leaves. They may be smooth ("entire"), finely toothed, coarsely toothed, or "double toothed" (each tooth combines a smaller and a larger tooth). The "teeth" may be rounded.

Other leaf characteristics

Several other distinctive characteristics of some trees with simple unlobed leaves also sometimes help identify the species:

- If the leaves flutter *very* actively in even a *very* slight breeze, it is an **Aspen** (p. 86) or possibly a **Gray Birch** (p. 90) or a **Cottonwood** (p. 99).
- If it is spring and the tree *already has leaves* when other trees are still bare, it is probably a **Willow** (p. 155). **Maples** (p. 114) also leaf out *relatively* early.
- If it is spring and the tree is *still largely bare* when other trees already have dense foliage, it is probably a **Sycamore** (p. 149; look for mottled

Describing Leaf Shapes

More-or-less roundish; width about equal to length

Ovate (egg-shaped, broader near base, about 1½–2 times longer than wide, curved at the base and tapering to a point at the tip)

Asymmetric (with significantly more leaf on one side of the central vein than on the other side)

More-or-less triangular

Oval (egg shaped, approximately same width at both ends), length more than 1.5 times width, curved at both ends)

Lanceolate (long and thin, with length 4 or more times the width

More-or-less heart-shaped ("cordate")

Obovate (egg-shaped, broader near the tip and narrow or pointed at the base)

Elliptical (oval but coming to a point at both ends)

Describing Leaf Edges

"entire" (smooth)

"finely toothed"

"coarsely toothed"

"double toothed"

Trees with Alternate, Simple, Unlobed Leaves			
Margin smooth (entire) or wavy	Oval to obovate or elongated ovate	Blocky bark; may have fine teeth near tip	**Black Tupelo**
		Distinctive chunky bark	**Persimmon**
	Heart shaped	Short, pointed tip	**Redbud**
Finely or moderately finely toothed margin	Roundish to ovate, with pointed tip	Long, flat petiole (stem). Leaves quiver in very slight breeze	**Quaking Aspen**
	Ovate (length generally about 1-2 times width)	Bark is white, peeling	**Paper Birch**
		Length about 1.5 times width; bark smooth, gray, sometimes vertically streaked	**Serviceberry**
		Short, stout trunk	**Apple**
		Long tapering point; small. shrubby tree	**American Plum**
		Bark is yellow-bronze, peeling	**Yellow Birch**
		Bark is gray or grayish black with cornflake-like scales	**Black Cherry**
	Lanceolate		**Willow**
Coarsely or bluntly toothed or double-toothed margin	Roundish to ovate, with bluntly pointed tip	Broadly wedge-shaped base; margins wavy or with broadly pointed teeth. Leaves quiver in very slight breeze	**Bigtooth Aspen**
		May be nearly heart-shaped; broken petiole (leaf stem) exudes milky sap	**Mulberry**

(continued)

Trees with Alternate, Simple, Unlobed Leaves			
Coarsely or bluntly toothed or double-toothed margin (continued)	Roundish to ovate, with bluntly pointed tip (continued)	Base is moderately or strongly asymmetric; teeth usually of 2 sizes; abruptly pointed tip. Prominent parallel veins.	**Elm**
		Leaves are stiff, dark glossy green, with spines along edges	**Holly**
		Long thorns on branches and twigs. Leaves may be lobed	**Hawthorns**
		Pointed tip and rounded base; whitish, peeling bark	**Paper Birch**
		May be asymmetric; bark yellowish bronze, peeling	**Yellow Birch**
		9-14 coarse teeth; smooth bark	**Beech**
	Ovate to elongated ovate (most leaves with length more than 2 times width	Fine teeth; bark is dark gray, thin, not peeling	**Black Birch**
		Length about 2 times width; wide, blunt, rounded teeth	**Chestnut Oak**
		Finely double toothed; bark is shaggy	**Hophornbeam**
		Finely double-toothed. Bark is blue-gray, smooth, "muscular"	**Hornbeam**

Trees with Alternate, Simple, Unlobed Leaves			
Coarsely or bluntly toothed or double-toothed margin (continued)	Ovate to elongated ovate (most leaves with length more than 2 times width)	Larger than 3" by 5" with short pointed tip; bark shallowly furrowed; grows in well-drained areas	**Basswood**
		Smaller than 3" by 5" with narrow, long, pointed tip; bark has rugged, deep furrows and ridges; grows in or near wetlands	**Cottonwood**
	Heart-shaped or triangular	Triangular with tip narrowly tapering to an elongated point; 1-4" long; bark is grayish-white with rough dark triangles or chevrons	**Gray Birch**
		Small (less than 3" long); bark pink to orange to reddish brown, peeling	**River Birch**

bark), a **Black Locust** (p. 112; look for very rugged, ropelike bark), or a **Black Cherry** (p. 97; look for bark with very dark, "cornflake-like" "scales).

- If it is early fall and the tree has *already lost its leaves* when most other trees still retain theirs, it may be an **Ash** (p. 81)
- If it is late fall and the tree *still has leaves* (green or turning yellow and red) when most other trees have dropped their leaves, it may be a **Sycamore** (p. 149), an **Oak** (p. 126), a **Norway Maple** (p. 116), or a **Willow** (p. 155).
- If the leaves are lobed, *alternately* arranged, and the bark is mottled and peels in large flat pieces, it is a **Sycamore**.
- If the leaves are lobed, *alternately* arranged, longer than wide, and the bark is not mottled or peeling in large flat pieces, it is an **Oak**.
- If the leaves are lobed, *oppositely* arranged, wider than they are long, and the bark is not mottled, it is a **Norway Maple**.
- If the leaves are very long and thin, it is a **Willow**.
- If it is late fall or winter and the tree still retains many of its (now-dried) leaves, it may be an **Oak** (p. 126), a **Beech** (p. 89), a **Hophornbeam** (p. 110), or a **Hornbeam** (p. 111).
- If the leaves are unlobed and the bark is smooth, it is a **Beech** (p. 89)
- If the leaves are unlobed, and the bark is smooth, it is an **Oak** (p. 126)
- If the leaves are unlobed and the bark is smooth but with a rippled or "muscular" look to it, it is an **Eastern Hophornbeam** (p. 110).
- If the leaves are unlobed and the bark is shaggy, it is a **Hornbeam** (p. 111)

IF IT IS A BROADLEAF TREE: USING BARK AS A FIELD MARK

Bark comes second only to leaves in identifying trees. In winter, when the leaves are absent, it is usually the starting point. However, even in winter, don't forget to check whether the small branches and leaf scars are arranged in an opposite or alternate pattern (see p. 11), and look for dead leaves on the ground under the tree. (Be careful: leaves can blow around). Then distinguish:

- Does the tree have thin bark or thick bark?
- What color is the bark?
- Is the bark generally smooth (though sometimes with lines or other marks or with sections peeling away from the trunk); or is it very rugged, with deep furrows and prominent ridges; or is it intermediate between these two?
- Are there distinctive marks on the bark? Sometimes these are patches of color. Or they may be *lenticels*—the openings through which

oxygen, carbon dioxide and water pass. Lenticels may take the form of horizontal lines or may be diamond-shaped or roundish.

- Does the bark have other distinctive characteristics, such as scales, or vertical stripes, or sections that are peeling?

Beware: Using bark alone to identify trees can be treacherous. A few trees have highly distinctive bark and can be identified by bark alone. But even with these, there are many variations.

Many young trees have bark that is smooth and grayish. The bark takes on the "classic" look shown in most guidebooks only when it is mature, and even then, there are major differences between individual trees of the same species. As the tree gets old, the bark may thicken and split, looking quite different than on the "mature" trees.

These photos are all of sugar maples, showing the aging of the bark, from the youngest on the left to the oldest on the right.

Also note that within a single species, and even among trees that are the same age, the bark on one tree may vary considerably from the bark on another. The bark may even look different on different parts of the same tree.

- Bark on the sunny side of the tree may differ from bark on the shady side.

shady side of a maple tree

sunny side of same tree

- Bark near the base of the tree may look different from bark higher up on the trunk or on the branches.

The bark field marks described below are typical, but not universal, for mature trees (i.e., trees that are neither very young nor very old).

Scarlet Oak lower trunk

Scarlet Oak upper trunk

Sycamore

Bigtooth Aspen trunk

Bigtooth Aspen upper limbs

Trees with thin bark

Trees with thin, smooth bark:

- If the bark is smooth and gray and the trunk forms a smooth (or sometimes slightly fluted) cylinder, it is a **Beech** (p. 89).
- If the bark is smooth and the trunk has a rippled or "muscular" quality, it is an **American Hornbeam** (p. 111).

Trees with thin, smooth bark with horizontal lines or other marks:

Many trees have prominent "lenticels"—pores through which water, oxygen, and carbon dioxide can pass—or other prominent markings. The size and shape of the lenticels can help identify the species.

Beech   Hornbeam

- If the bark is dark reddish brown to gray (sometimes dark gray), generally smooth but marked by prominent *horizontal lenticels*, and the leaves are ovate with fine, sharp, double teeth on the edges, it is a **Black Birch** (p. 91).
- If the bark is chalky white and generally smooth, but marked by dark triangles or chevrons, and *not* peeling away from the trunk, and the tree has long, triangular, double toothed leaves, it is a **Gray Birch** (p. 91).

Black Birch bark   Black Birch leaf   Gray Birch bark   Gray Birch leaf

Quaking Aspen bark — lower   Quaking Aspen bark — upper   Quaking Aspen leaf

- If the bark is whitish with roundish or diamond-shaped lenticels and the leaves are nearly round with *small teeth*, it is a **Quaking Aspen** (p. 87). The "whitish" bark may be visible only on the upper limbs. The bark on the *lower* part of the trunk or the entire trunk of mature trees may also be whitish, or it may be grayish-tan or dark and furrowed and the lenticels may be fused.
- If the bark is light tan to yellowish- to greenish-gray, with *diamond-shaped* marks or short lines, and the leaves are roundish to ovoid, with *large, blunt teeth*, it is a **Bigtooth Aspen** (p. 86). The "white" part of the bark may be sharply reduced: The bark on the lower part of the trunk of older trees may be dark grayish brown with interlacing

Bigtooth Aspen bark — lower   Bigtooth Aspen bark — upper   Bigtooth Aspen leaf

flattened ridges; paler inner bark may be visible in furrows, but the bark of upper branches remains light.

Trees with thin and generally smooth bark but with many areas peeling away from the trunk in curling, horizontal curls:

- If the bark is whitish, with double toothed, ovate leaves with a pointed tip, it is a **Paper Birch** (p. 92)

Paper Birch bark   Paper Birch leaf

- If the bark is yellowish or bronze or silvery-gray, with ovate, finely toothed leaves, it is a **Yellow Birch** (p. 93). Yellow Birch is especially likely to be found in moist sites or near wetlands.

Yellow Birch bark   Yellow Birch leaf

River Birch bark River Birch leaf

- If the bark is salmon-pink to reddish-brown with much lighter inner bark, and triangular, coarsely double-toothed leaves, it is a River Birch (p. 93). River Birch is especially likely to be found in or near wetlands.

Trees with very rugged bark

If the tree has *very* rugged bark, with *very* deep furrows and *very* prominent, intricately interlocking, *ropelike* vertical ridges, and compound leaves with oval leaflets, it is a **Black Locust** (p. 112).

Black Locust bark Black Locust leaf

If the bark is made up of very rugged, vertical, elongated, *blocklike* chunks with each block typically 4 or 5 times longer than wide, and the leaves are

Chestnut Oak bark   Chestnut Oak leaf

elongated ovals with very coarse, *rounded* teeth or shallow lobes, it is a **Chestnut Oak** (p. 137).

If the bark is deeply furrowed, with vertical, *blocklike* chunks (each block typically about twice as long as wide), it is a **Black Tupelo** (p. 151).

Black Tupelo bark   Black Tupelo leaf

If the bark is dark gray-brown and divided into squarish, scaly, thick plates (sometimes described as looking like charcoal briquettes), it is a **Persimmon** (p. 144).

Several other tree species also have rugged bark but the bark is less distinctive. These trees are most easily distinguished by their leaves.

Persimmon bark   Persimmon leaf

If the leaves are lobed and are vaguely "tulip- shaped," with no point at either end and a flat or shallowly notched tip, it is a **Tuliptree** (p. 150).

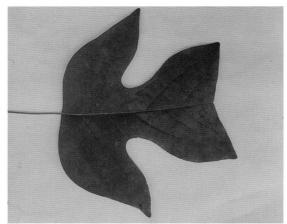

Tuliptree bark   Tuliptree leaf

If the leaves are lobed and many are "fiddle-shaped," with a very narrow section in the lower middle part of the leaf, it is a **Bur (Mossy Cup) Oak** (p. 133). Look for corky "wings" on smaller branches.

If the leaves are more or less triangular or heart-shaped, and the tree is found in a wet field or by a pond or stream bank, it is a **Cottonwood** (p. 99).

Bur Oak twig

Bur Oak leaf

Bur Oak bark

Cottonwood bark

Cottonwood leaf

Other trees with distinctive bark

A number of other species are best described as having "distinctive" bark.

If the bark shows a diamond or alligator-skin like pattern, especially near the base, and has oppositely arranged compound leaves, it is an **Ash** trees (p. 81).

If the tree looks like it is covered by blackish "cornflakes" or "potato chips," it is a **Black Cherry** (p. 97).

If the bark is made up of small, regularly arranged square plates and the tree has oppositely arranged, smooth-edged leaves, it is a **Dogwood** (p. 100).

White Ash bark

White Ash leaf

Black Cherry bark

Black Cherry leaf

Dogwood bark

Dogwood leaf

Serviceberry (p. 147): Small flowers with long white petals.

Elm (p. 101): Small yellow and pinkish/purplish flowers clustered along the twigs.

Early flowering trees with "catkins"

The flowers on some trees take the form of "catkins"—long, slim, cylindrical clusters of tiny flowers, somewhat downy and reminiscent of a cat's tail)

Trees with catkins that appear in mid-Spring, before the leaves:

Gray Birch (p. 91) and **River Birch** (p. 93): Yellow or yellowish-green catkins, 1"–2" long. (**Black Birch**, **Paper Birch**, and **Yellow Birch** catkins do not appear until somewhat later in spring, when many trees are already leaving out.) Distinguish the elongated, drooping male birch catkins, 8–10 times as long as they are wide, from the erect female birch catkins, 2–4 times as long as they are wide.

Cottonwood (p. 99): Greenish or reddish-brown catkins, 3"–4" long.

Willows (p. 155): Yellow or yellowish-green catkins, up to 2" long.

Trees that have conspicuous flowers that appear after the leaves have come out

Trees with conventional flowers appearing after leaves include:

Basswood (p. 88): Hanging clusters of fragrant, creamy yellow flowers. The stem is attached for part of its length to a long, leaflike "bract." The fruits, when they form, remain attached to the bracts and may remain on the tree well into winter.

Catalpa (p. 96): Clusters of large (2"–2.25") white, bell-shaped flowers with yellow and purple spots. Look for large, heart-shaped leaves.

Black Cherry (p. 97): Drooping, 2"–4" long clusters of white flowers. Look for dark bark making the tree look like it is covered by black cornflakes.

Hawthorn (p. 104): Branching clusters of 10–20 white flowers, each about ⅝" wide. Look for a shrub or very small tree.

Basswood flower

Catalpa flower

Black Cherry flower

Horse Chestnut (p. 112): 4"–6" by 8"–10" upright, cone-shaped aggregates of white flowers. Look for palmately compound leaves.

Black Locust (p. 112): Clusters of showy white flowers. Look for pinnately compound leaves and very rugged bark.

Nannyberry Flower (p. 125): 2"–4" wide clusters of tiny (¼") white flowers in late spring. Look for a shrub or very small tree.

American Plum (p. 144): White flowers, about 1" diameter, singly or in clusters where the stem and a leaf meet. Fragrant but with an unpleasant odor. Look for a small tree or shrub.

Tuliptree (p. 150): Yellow, tulip-shaped flowers. Look for squarish, lobed leaves.

Hawthorn flower

Horse Chestnut flower

Black Locust flower

Nannyberry flower

American Plum flower

Tuliptree flower

Trees with catkins appearing mid or late spring, after the leaves appear

Beech (p. 89): Yellow-green. Look for smooth, grayish bark.

Black Birch (p. 91), **Paper Birch** (p. 93), and **Yellow Birch** (p. 93): Yellow or yellowish-green. Look for thin bark with horizontal lenticels, peeling away from the trunk in the case of Paper Birch and Yellow Birch.

Hickories (p. 105): Reddish green or yellowish green. Look for pinnately compound leaves.

Hophornbeam (p. 110): Reddish brown or yellowish green. Look for shaggy bark.

Hornbeam (p. 111): Green. Look for smooth grayish bark with a twisted or "muscular" look.

Oaks (p. 126): Yellowish-green. In rows, like a curtain. Look for lobed leaves.

Black Walnut (p. 152): Green. Look for pinnately compound leaves.

Trees that have flowers that don't appear until late fall or early winter, or that persist in dried form into winter

Witch Hazel (p. 156), a shrub or small tree, has small yellow flowers appearing in late fall.

Birches (p. 90) and **Hophornbeams** (p. 110) retain their now-brown or reddish-brown catkins in fall and winter after the leaves have fallen off.

Witch Hazel flowers

Birch fall catkin

SEEDS AND FRUITS

Seeds and fruits may be found on the tree or on the ground under the tree.

The seeds of trees may take any of several forms. Some are nuts (a seed enclosed in a hard or leathery shell; an acorn is a nut borne in a woody cap formed from the base of the flower). Others are samaras—single seeds enclosed in a hard shell and carried in a flattened, papery wing, which may fall to the ground or be blown some distance by the wind. Yet others drop their seeds enclosed in a pod or enclosed in fleshy berries or in other forms of fruit.

Acorns

If the tree has *acorns* on the tree or found on the ground under the tree, it is an **Oak** (p. 126). The size, shape, and how much of the acorn is covered by the cap can help distinguish among the oaks.

Acorns

Other nuts

Trees that bear *nuts* on the tree or found on the ground under the tree (often encased in a woody outer shell or husk) include:

Hickories (p. 105). ⅔"–2" diameter nuts, green on the tree, turning brown or dark brown. The size and shape and the thickness of the husk can help distinguish among hickories.

 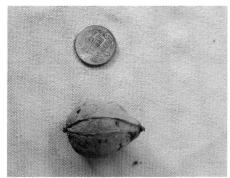

Hickory nuts

Beech nut   Butternut   Black Walnut

Beech (p. 89): Pairs of small, triangular nuts in a soft-spined, 4 lobed, ½"–¾" woody husk.

Butternut (White Walnut; p. 95) and Black Walnut (p. 152): Roundish nuts, the size of a golf ball or larger, seen on the tree or on the ground under the tree. Butternut nuts are slightly elongated with a blunt point and are sticky to the touch. Black Walnut nuts are round and not sticky.

Samaras

A samara (sometimes called a "key") is a thin, paperlike fruit surrounding a seed. The winglike casing helps the seed to be carried away by the wind. Samaras may have a single wing with the seed near one end, or two wings, or be more-or-less oval with the seed at the center or have other shapes. They are often found on the ground under the tree or may be seen hanging in clusters on the tree.

Single winged samaras
    Ashes (p. 81)

Two-winged samaras
    Maples (p. 114)

Oval samaras
    Elms (p. 103)

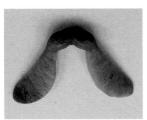

White Ash samara   Red Maple samara

Elm samara

Other samaras

Ailanthus (p. 80): Dense clusters of twisted, single-winged samaras

American Hornbeam (p. 111): Seeds are surrounded by a three-lobed, 2–3 cm diameter bract, positioned like an umbrella over the seeds, and arranged in dense, droopy clusters.

Tuliptrees (p. 150): conelike aggregates of samaras, persisting on the tree in dried form into winter. From a distance, the opened-up aggregates look like a tulip.

Alianthus samara

Tuliptree fruit

Hornbeam samara

Tuliptree fruits on tree

Pods

Pods are elongated containers with two halves that can split open, revealing the seeds. Trees bearing their seeds in pods include:

Black Locust (p. 112): Flattened pods, 2"–4" long, late summer to fall, which may persist into winter.

Catalpa (p. 96): Long (8"–20"), slender, beanlike pods; green turning dark brown, persisting through the winter

Redbud (p. 145): Flattened, dry, brown, 2"–4" flat pods.

Black Locust seed pods   Catalpa seed pods   Redbud seed pods

Berries

Trees with *berries* include **Black Cherry** (round fruits, about ⅓" diameter, near-black when ripe, p. 97); **Black Tupelo**, (ovoid fruits, about ⅔" long, dark blue, p. 151); and **Dogwood** (clusters of bright red ⅓"–½" ovoid berries, p. 100). The bark will easily distinguish among these. **Mulberry** has blackberry-like fruits, about 1" long, pale turning red and then purplish (p. 124).

Shrubs and small trees with berries include **Nannyberry** (clusters of ⅓"–½" bluish-black berries, which may persist into winter, p. 125); and **Winterberry** (red berries, which also remain on the tree well into winter, p. 155).

Dogwood

Black Cherry

Black Tupelo

Mulberry

Winterberry

Nannyberry

Apple   American Plum   Wahoo

Sycamore buttonball

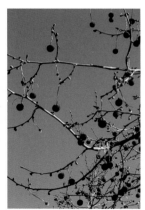

Sycamore buttonballs on tree

Other fruits

Apple (p. 81): The apple of commerce—round or slightly ellipsoid, green turning red when ripe, 2"–4" diameter.

American Plum (p. 144): Red to yellow, globular when ripe, about 1" in diameter.

Sycamore (p. 149): Spherical, tightly packed, clusters of seeds ("buttonballs"), tan-to-brown, about 1" diameter.

Eastern Wahoo (p. 152): 4-lobed seed capsules, each ½" across, red to purple, containing 1–2 seeds.

BUDS

In winter, the terminal (end) buds of trees can be very helpful in identifying the species. A few trees can often be identified by their distinctive buds, alone. Even when the buds are not especially distinctive, they can often help you determine which of several closely related species you have found. This is especially useful with oaks.

Multiple terminal buds
Oaks (p. 126)

Red Oak bud

White Oak bud

Ruby-red buds
Basswood (p. 88)

Red Maple (p. 117)

Slender, spindle-shaped buds

Beech (p. 89)

Onion-shaped buds
(globular, flattened on the bottom, slightly pointed at the top):
Dogwood (p. 100).

Elongated, yellow buds   Round buds with a long, pointed tip
  Bitternut Hickory (p. 105)   **Nannyberry** (p. 125)

THORNS

The presence of thorns on the trunk or on smaller branches and twigs makes a few trees immediately identifiable. **Black Locust** (p. 112) has a pair of small (less than ½") thorns at the base of leaves.

Hawthorns (p. 104) have large (often more than 1") thorns on their branches (and sometimes on the trunk, as well).

TREE IDENTIFICATION—FIELD CHECKLIST

Date: _____ Location: _____

Habitat: Dry ☐   Wet field or wetland ☐   Edge of pond or stream ☐
       Open area/meadow ☐   At edge of woods ☐   In the woods ☐   Sunny ☐
       Part shade ☐   Shady ☐

Overall form:
Size: (Height, diameter of trunk) _____

Shape? How high up on trunk do branches start? _____

Branches horizontal? ascending? drooping? _____

Leaves:
Needles or needlelike ☐
Broadleaf ☐
Opposite ☐   Alternate ☐
Lobed ☐   Unlobed ☐   (If lobed, describe or sketch): _____
Simple ☐   Pinnately compound ☐   Palmately compound ☐
Edges: Smooth ☐   Fine teeth ☐   Coarse teeth ☐   Double toothed ☐

Color: Top surface: _____ Underside: _____

Leaves smooth or hairy: Top surface _____ Underside _____

Bark:
Color: _____
Smooth ☐   Peeling ☐   Shaggy ☐   Very rugged ☐   In between ☐
Describe ridges (flat? scaly? irregular? Or forming pattern?) _____

Other characteristics:
Buds: Shape: _____ Size: _____ Color: _____
Surface: Smooth ☐   Slightly hairy ☐   Very hairy ☐

Twigs: Color: _____ Texture (rough/smooth; hairy; etc.) _____

Flowers: Color _____ Form: _____
Fruits: Acorn ☐   Other Nut ☐   Samara ☐   Pod ☐   Berry ☐   Other ☐
Describe (including size, color): _____
Thorns ☐
Dead leaves remaining on the tree in winter ☐

Comments: _____

Identification of tree: _____

Part II: The Native Trees of Connecticut

The individual species of trees are described below: first conifers, separated into sections on Pines, Firs and Spruces, and Other Conifers; then broadleaf trees organized alphabetically by individual species or by the English name of the *genus* (a group of closely related species) when there are several trees of that *genus* present (e.g., all maples, including Boxelder, are grouped under "maples").

The book describes the overall shape and form, leaves, bark, and habitat for each species of tree native to Connecticut. Other characteristics (e.g., buds in winter, flowers, fruits and nuts) are described only when they can be easily used to help identify the tree.

The "Shape and Form" sections below describes trees grown in the open. Trees growing in the middle of the woods tend to have long, upright trunks with few branches, and a crown only high up.

CONIFERS

There are three major groups of conifers in Connecticut: the pines, recognizable by their long, thin clusters of needles; the firs and spruces, recognized by their shorter, denser needles; and a miscellaneous group including cedars, hemlocks, and tamaracks.

pine   fir   cedar

PINES

The pines are usually easily distinguished from other confers by their long, thin, soft needles. The needles grow in clusters of 2, 3, or 5 from a common origin point on a branch. The ground around the trees is covered with fallen needles. The branches of the tree grow in whorls at the same level of the tree, They may be more-or-less horizontal in orientation or irregular. Pinecones hang downward. The scales that make them up are stiff and woody. Entire cones fall off the tree and are commonly found on the ground. The number of cones a pine produces vary widely from year to year. A number of other species, including hickories, beeches, maples, spruces, and oaks show a similar pattern, which is described in more detail under "oaks" (p. 00).

Distinguishing Among the Pines			
Species	**Bark**	**Needles**	**Cones**
White Pine	Grayish, horizontally-cracked scales separating from trunk at edges. Older trees have thick, irregular, jigsaw puzzlelike scales.	Clusters of *five* 2.5"–5" long needles, soft, and thin, arrayed all along twig on all sides of twig. Needles at end of twig droop a bit.	Long, slightly curved ellipsoids, 4"–8" long, with long stalk.
Pitch Pine	Irregularly rectangular; reddish-brown to grayish-brown plates separated by fissures.	Clusters of *three* 3"–5" long needles, sharply pointed, stiff, often in a puffball-like array at the end of twig or growing directly out of the trunk.	Plump, 1"–3" long, with short, stiff downturned prickles at ends of scales. Often clustered and may remain attached to tree for several years after ripening.
Red Pine	Thick, with light reddish-brown, irregularly rectangular, thin, scaly plates broken by fissures.	Clusters of *two* 2"–6" long needles, relatively brittle, arrayed on all sides of twig and all along twig.	Egg shaped, less than 2" long, solitary or in pairs.

EASTERN WHITE PINE
Pinus Strobus

Look For: *Five soft, blue-green, long needles per cluster; long (up to 8") cones; thick, dark, brownish bark.*

Shape and Form: A tall tree with a straight trunk and a broadly conical crown (becoming irregular with age). Branches horizontal or curving upwards.

Bark: Smooth, greenish-gray in younger trees, turning grayish-brown and then darkening further, with grayish, horizontal finely cracked scales separating from trunk at edges. Older trees have almost-black, thick, irregular, jigsaw puzzle-like scales. With increasing age, furrows deepen. Twigs are smooth, pale reddish-brown.

Needles: The only five-needled pine in the US (Mnemonic: five needles "white" has five letters). Needles are light- to bluish-green, soft and thin, triangular in cross section, 2.5"–5" long, and are faintly striped by fine lines of white dots (lenticels) along the needles. Needles are arranged all along the twig, rather than in lollipop-like clusters (as with pitch pine). Looked at from the end of the branchlets, the lower needles droop down, forming an array with a much longer "radius" at the bottom than at the top.

Cones: Up to 4"–8" long ellipsoids, with 0.4"–1.0" long stalk, slightly curved; margins of scales paler than the brown body of the cone.

Habitat: Prefers well drained, moist soils.

Wildlife Use: Dense foliage and whorled limbs provide good winter cover and protection against cold and good nesting sites for many birds. Nests of larger birds (including wild turkeys) tend to be near the trunk, with nests of smaller birds further out. All parts of the tree provide food: The twigs and foliage are the most palatable of the pines to large herbivores. Seeds are eaten by many species—squirrels, chipmunks, mice, grosbeaks, nuthatches, chickadees, pine siskins, woodpeckers, and others. Rabbits and porcupines eat the inner bark.

Comments: The whorls of branches can be used to tell the age of the tree: One year for each whorl.

White Pine was the foremost timber tree of colonial America and is still one of the most important lumber trees in the East. The long, straight trunks were prized for ship masts in colonial times. The trees also provided the wood for planking, pitch and tar, and turpentine. The trees were so valuable that King George I declared large white pines to be the property of the King, no matter whose land they grew on. Royal agents traveled throughout New England, marking out the trees they wanted with the "King's broad arrow"—three axe strikes, two forming the arrowhead, the third the shaft. Colonists also wanted the trees, for houses, furniture, and other products. The conflict led to active resistance and armed skirmishes, including the "White Pine War" and the "Pine Tree Riot" of 1772. Some historians claim that the King's effort to monopolize the pines was as important as taxation of tea in bringing about the rebellion against the Crown that ended up as the American Revolution. The first colonial flag, flown at the Battle of Bunker Hill, bore an Eastern White Pine as emblem. Later "Pine Tree" flags, emblazoned with the words "An Appeal to Heaven," were an expression of the right of revolution.

PITCH PINE
Pinus rigida
Look For: *Three stiff, twisted needles per cluster; 3"–5" long, egg-shaped cones; yellow-brown plated bark. May have tufts of needles growing out of trunk.*

Shape and Form: A medium-sized tree with a straight trunk, tufts of needles along trunk, and a rounded or irregular crown.

Bark: Irregularly rectangular reddish-brown to dark, slightly purplish, gray-brown plates separated by fissures. Plates grow away from trunk at top and bottom. In older trees, plates thicken and flatten. Twigs are orange-brown to dark brown.

Needles: 3–5" long, sharply pointed, stiff needles, in clusters of three. (Mnemonic: "Pitch"— "Three strikes you're out"). Needles are arranged on all sides of the twig, often in lollipop-like clusters. Looked at from the end of the branchlets, they form a circular array. Unlike other pines, Pitch Pine needles may grow in tufts of needles directly out of the trunk.

Cones: Plump, 1–3" cm long, with short, stiff downturned prickles at ends of scales. Often clustered and may remain attached for several years after ripening.

Habitat: Prefers thin or sandy, dry to boggy soils. Shade intolerant.

Wildlife Use: A valuable nesting and cover tree for songbirds and raptors. Seeds remain protected in the cones and are not very available as food, but may be eaten by mice, chipmunks, nuthatches, grosbeaks, and chickadees.

RED PINE (NORWAY PINE)
Pinus resinosa

Look For: *Two long needles per cluster; bark with red, scaly plates; short (2") cones the shape of a small hen's egg.*

Shape and Form: A medium-sized tree with a straight trunk and narrowly rounded or irregular crown.

Bark: Thick, with light reddish-brown, irregularly rectangular, thin, scaly plates, broken by shallow fissures. Upper trunk and limbs light reddish-orange. Twigs orange- to red-brown.

Needles: 2"–6" long, deep yellow-green, in clusters of two, arrayed on all sides all along twig; looked at from the end they form a circular array, though more sparsely needled than pitch pine. Fresh needles are brittle and break cleanly when bent double.

Cones: Egg shaped; solitary or in pairs; less than 2" long; light reddish-brown; nearly stalkless.

Habitat: Tolerates sandy acid soils better than white pine, but also found on margins of swamps. Will grow in shade, but slowly.

Wildlife Use: Relatively sparse limbs and long needles make red pines not conducive to nest placement, save by larger bird species. The tree does provide winter cover and protection against the cold. Small mammals and songbirds eat the seeds. Red Pine is listed by the Connecticut Department of Energy and Environmental Protection (DEEP) as being "endangered."

Comments: The name "Norway Pine" refers to the Maine village of Norway, not the country.

FIRS AND SPRUCES

Both firs and spruces have shorter needles than the pines, growing all around the twigs, but firs and spruces are easily confused.

The number of cones a tree produces vary widely from year to year. Several other species, including pines, hickories, beeches, maples, and oaks show a similar pattern, which is described in more detail under "oaks" (p. 126).

BALSAM FIR
Abies balsamea

Look For: *Soft, flat needles (hard to roll between your fingers); upward-turned cones at top of tree (and not on ground). Tree is conical with a narrowed, spirelike top.*

Shape and Form: A small to medium tree with a conical crown narrowing to a spire. The branches extend from the trunk in regular whorls.

Bark: Relatively smooth bark, gray, with small, short horizontal lenticels and raised bumps. In older trees, rougher, cracked, forming irregular shallow blocks or scales. Lower branches are wide, upright to horizontal.

Needles: 0.5"–1.0" long, dark, rich green, flattened. Sides of needles are almost parallel for entire length and tips may be notched or rounded or flat. (Hemlock needles, with which they might be confused, are wider at base and taper to rounded top). Two greenish white bands made up of tiny dots (lenticels) are on lower surface. Needles near middle of twig are longest. On upper branches, needles are arranged all around the stem; on lower branches they may be arranged more or less horizontally on opposite sides of the stem, giving a flattened overall appearance. Twigs are pale gray and have a sweet odor. Overall,

Distinguishing Firs from Spruces				
	Overall shape	Needles	Cones	Bark
Firs	• Narrow conical crown, narrowing to a spire at the top • Branches ascend or are horizontal	• Grow as individual needles on all sides of a stem • Dark, rich green, with 2 greenish white bands on lower surface. • Notched or rounded tip • Needles feel soft and are flat in cross-section. It is hard to roll them between your fingers • Needles near middle of twig are longest • Broken off needles leave behind a smooth twig with small circular leaf scars. • Have a sweet odor	• 2"–3" long, elliptical, purple or green, turning brown. • Cones grow upward, like candle flames, and are found mainly near the top of the tree. • Cones fall off the tree in pieces, so there are few entire cones on the ground underneath the tree.	• Relatively smooth gray bark, forming irregular shallow blocks or scales in older trees. Small, dashlike lenticels and small raised bumps may be evident. • Twigs are pale gray

Distinguishing Firs from Spruces				
	Overall shape	Needles	Cones	Bark
Spruces	Trees usually have more or less conical form	• Grow as individual needles along all sides of a stem • Mossy-green • Sharply pointed tip • Needles feel brittle and prickly and are square or diamond-shaped in cross section. It is relatively easy to roll them between your fingers • Needles along twig are of even size • Needles are attached to a golf tee–shaped structure. When needles are shed, pegs remain and twig feels rough. • Have a slightly peppery odor	• Cones tend to have a smooth and flexible shape, with thin scales • Cones hang downward, towards the ground. • Entire cones fall off tree and are found on the ground under the tree	• Rough and flaky/scaly bark • Twigs are orange

the needles give the tree a "furry" feel.

Cones: 0.75"–1.25" diameter, 2"–3" long, elliptical, purple or green, turning brown. Grow upward, like candle flames. Mainly found near top of tree.

Habitat: Moist, cool woodlands and swamps, often in mixed stands with other conifers and hardwoods. Very shade tolerant.

Wildlife Use: The foliage is not very palatable to deer, who will browse but do not prefer firs. The buds are eaten by squirrels, the seeds by a variety of birds.

Comments: Because of its fragrance and symmetry, firs are popular as Christmas trees. Fir is a major pulpwood species. The blisters on the trunk produce a resin used for mounting microscopic specimens. Balsam Fir is listed on the Connecticut Department of Energy and Environmental Protection (DEEP) list as being "endangered."

SPRUCES

Genus Picea

Bark: Bark is rough and flaky/scaly. Twigs are orange to brown.

Needles: Spruce needles grow as individual needles along all sides of a stem. They are more-or-less square in cross section, making them relatively easy to roll them between your fingers. The needles are attached to the twig by a peg-like structure; when the needles are shed, the pegs remain and the twig feels rough. The length of the needles and whether their tips are blunt or pointed can help identify the species (see below).

Cones: Egg-shaped or cylindrical cones, smooth with thin scales, hanging towards the ground. Cones fall off the tree and can be found on the ground under the tree. The characteristics of the cones can be used to help identify the species of Spruce (see below).

Wildlife Use: Spruces, with their dense branches, provide excellent winter cover for songbirds and mammals and nesting sites for birds, including woodpeckers, thrushes, warblers, and finches. Deer will browse the foliage in winter, though spruces are not a preferred species. Woodpeckers, chickadees, nuthatches, finches, and other songbirds eat the seeds.

Comments: The wood of Red Spruce and Norway Spruce is both stiff and light, the ideal properties for transmitting the vibrations of stringed instruments to the air. As a result, it is widely used for violins, high end guitars, and the sound boards of pianos.

Red, Black, and White Spruces can be difficult to distinguish from one another.

- White Spruce needles tend to be the longest (0.5"–0.75" long), yellowish to bluish green. The often-curved needles are relatively far apart from one another. Cones are 1.25"–2.5" long, elongated.
- Red Spruce needles are 0.5"–0.6" long, green, and tend to point towards the end of the twig. Cones are 1.25"–1.5" long, somewhat elongated.
- Black Spruce needles tend to be the shortest (0.25"–0.6" long), dullish bluish green, relatively short, and fairly straight. The roundish cones are very small (less than 1" long).
- The Norway Spruce needles are flatter and longer (0.5"–1.25") than those of the other spruces. Cones are 4"–6" long.
- To complicate matters, Red and Black Spruces easily hybridize and intermediate forms are often seen.

BLACK SPRUCE
Picea mariana
A small spruce with an irregularly conical crown and often a clump of branches at the top; relatively short (0.25"–0.6" long), stiff, usually blunt tipped needles (dull blue-green, sometimes with a waxy bloom); and very small (less than 1.25" long), roundish cones, often clustered near top of the tree. Bark has an olive or yellow-green hue beneath the scales. Young twigs are yellow-brown to brown, often covered with small rusty to black hairs.

Black spruce

NORWAY SPRUCE
Picea abies
Conical crown; needles 0.5"–1.0" long, pointed, dark green, on conspicuously downwardly drooping branchlets; very long (4"–6"), cylindrical cones. Needles tend to point towards end of twig. Needles are somewhat flatter than those of other spruces and are harder to roll between the fingers.

Norway Spruce is not native to Connecticut but is widely cultivated and has naturalized very widely.

RED SPRUCE
Picea rubens
Moderately broad, conical crown; medium length (0.5"–0.7" long), yellow-green to dark green, shiny, pointed needles; and medium-small (1.25"–2.0" long), oval, somewhat elongated cones. Bark has a reddish hue beneath the scales. Young twigs are reddish to orange-brown, covered with rusty to black hairs.

WHITE SPRUCE
(Picea glauca)
Conical crown; relatively long (0.5"–0.75" long), sharp pointed, bluish-green to dark green needles, often waxy, and 1.25"–2.5" long elongated cones hanging at ends of twigs. The young twigs are light gray to yellowish brown, but unlike Red and Black Spruce, they are not hairy.

Distinguishing Among the Spruces				
Species and overall form	**Bark and Twigs**	**Needles**	**Cones**	**Habitat**
Black Spruce Crown often irregular with short, drooping branches that may curve up at ends, or thin and columnlike, with a dense clump of branches at the top	Thin, gray-brown, with irregular, fine, flaky scales. Newly exposed bark is olive or yellowish green. Twigs are yellow brown to brown, covered by short, rusty to black hairs, which may rub off as twigs age.	0.25"–0.6" long, rigid, dullish blue-green, blunt pointed, flexible and soft to the touch, square in cross section and easy to roll between fingers. Some needles may be waxy. Crushed needles have slight medicinal, menthol smell.	Short (0.75"–1.25"), egg-shaped, dark purple turning dull grayish-brown, with thin, woody, brittle, minutely toothed upper margins. Cones often remain attached in clusters near the top of the tree.	Most common on moist, poorly drained soils on the borders of swamps
Red Spruce Crown a moderately broad cone with spreading, horizontal branches	Reddish-brown to gray-brown, with irregular, flaky scales; furrowed on older trees. Newly exposed bark is reddish brown. Reddish brown twigs have short, rusty to black hairs in grooves between bases of needles.	0.5"–0.7" long, shiny dark yellow-green to dark green, square in cross section and easy to roll between fingers, sharply pointed, not waxy, point towards tip of branch. Crushed needles have slight citrus odor.	Elongated (1.25"–2.0"), bluish-green turning orange-brown, with thin, woody, brittle, smooth or irregularly toothed upper margins. Cones fall from tree at maturity.	Cool, well-drained, rocky upland areas. Shade tolerant.

(continued)

Distinguishing Among the Spruces				
Norway Spruce Crown a cone. The thickly leaved smaller branchlets droop conspicuously, often to the ground.	Orange-brown becoming gray-brown; scaly in older trees. Newly exposed bark is salmon colored. Twigs are orangish brown, hairless.	0.5"–1.0" long, rigid, shiny light to dark green, pointed, diamond-shaped (hard to roll between fingers).	Very elongated (4"–6" long), cylindrical with a conical tip; scales diamond-shaped	Non-native but widely naturalized and widely distributed
White Spruce Crown a cone or irregular with broad base, relatively thick horizontal branches, curved upward.	Younger trees smooth, light gray. Older trees, gray to brown with irregular, platelike scales; yellowish in fissures. Twigs are light gray to yellowish brown, and hairless.	0.5"–0.75" long, dullish yellowish to bluish green, sharp pointed, rigid, square in cross section and easy to roll between fingers. Some needles may be waxy. On the lower half of the twig, needles may curve upward so that all are on upper side. Bruised needles have unpleasant odor.	1.25"–2.5" long, an elongated tapered cylinder, light brown	Adaptable. Shade intolerant. Found mainly in northern part of Connecticut.

OTHER CONIFERS

If a tree is a conifer and you have ruled out its being one of the pines, fir, or a spruce, it is a cedar, hemlock, or a tamarack.

EASTERN RED CEDAR
Juniperus virginiana

Look For: *Fibrous bark; needles growing all around twigs; and grayish-blue, berrylike cones.*

Shape and Form: Small to medium-sized tree with a dense crown. Crown may be upright and narrowly columnar or spirelike or broadly conical or rounded, and bushy. The uppermost shoot may be bent over.

Bark: Reddish-brown to gray, fibrous, peeling off in thin, vertical strips. Strips may be oriented in a slight spiral.

Needles: Green to bluish-green. The leaves take two forms: younger leaves are needlelike and sharply pointed, up to 0.6" long. Older (and more common) leaves are made up of tiny, tightly overlapping scales. Needles grow all around twigs and the sprigs are not especially flattened.

Cones: Fleshy merged scales give the cones a berrylike appearance. Bluish, with a white, powdery looking, waxy coating, about 0.25"–.04" diameter. The larger (up to 1"), roundish, "cedar apples" that are sometimes found on the branches are not cones, but growths resulting from the attack of a fungus.

Habitat: Adaptable but more common in dry, sandy soils and rocky ridges in forest interiors.

Wildlife Use: A common pioneer species in cleared areas. The dense foliage provides nesting sites and cover for many songbirds and game birds. The seeds are a high value food for cedar waxwings, grosbeaks, and other song and game birds. (The cedar waxwing was given its name because of its fondness for the berries). Having its seeds eaten benefits the tree: Seeds that are exposed to

the birds' digestive processes and then excreted are three times more likely to germinate than seeds that fall directly to the ground.

Comments: Although the berries are used in some food preparations, this is not the juniper berry used for making gin; in excess it can be toxic. Cedar Oil for medicine comes from the wood and leaves. The aromatic red heartwood and whitish or yellowish sapwood repels moths and is often used for cedar chests and closet interiors.

NORTHERN WHITE CEDAR (ARBORVITAE)
Thuja occidentalis

Look For: *Small, scalelike needles in flattened, fan-shaped, yellow-green sprays; tiny brown woody upright cones; light gray bark with vertical, somewhat shreddy strips.*

Shape and Form: Small to medium-sized tree, with a compact, narrowly pyramidal, or broadly conical crown and horizontal branches extending to the ground. Trunk often twisted and sometimes divided into two or more secondary trunks.

Bark: Thin, fibrous, red-brown to gray-brown, peeling in long, thin, vertical strips. Strips may be oriented in a slight spiral.

Needles: Made up of tiny, slightly yellowish-green, tightly overlapping scales on slightly reddish-brown branchlets in a flattened, fan-shaped array. The scales are larger than those of Atlantic White Cedar.

Cones: Tiny (0.3"–0.6" long), dull yellow-green maturing to brown, somewhat elongated ovoid, woody, found upright at ends of branches.

Habitat: Adaptable. Commonly found in wet areas. Moderately shade tolerant.

Wildlife Use: Provides wind-break, protection from cold, and bark to feed on for deer that gather in white cedar swamps in winter. Pine siskins, red polls, red squirrels, and others feed on the seeds. Limb and needle arrangement are not especially favorable for building nests, but squirrels use strips of the outer bark in their nests.

Comments: The vitamin C in a tea made from the bark saved early French explorers from scurvy, who gave the tree its Latin name, *arborvitae* ("tree of life"). American Indians used the lightweight, easily split wood for canoe frames. Northern White Cedar is listed by the Connecticut Department of Energy and Environmental Protection (DEEP) as being "threatened."

ATLANTIC WHITE CEDAR
Chamaecyparis thyoides

Look For: *Flattened fanlike springs of "needles" made up of tiny, flat, overlapping, pointed scales, and fibrous bark.*

Shape and Form: Small to medium-sized tree with a dense, narrow, pointed, spirelike crown and short, horizontal, or ascending branches. In mature trees, much of the trunk is bare and the crown only begins three quarters of the way up on the trunk.

Bark: Reddish-brown turning ashy-gray, with flaky or fibrous, vertical strips that peel away from the trunk.

Needles: Opposite pairs of slightly bluish-green needles, made up of tiny, tightly overlapping scales. On the finest branchlets, the needles form a flattened array, but the several fine branchlets are arrayed in all directions, so overall, the arrays do not appear flattened.

Cones: Very small (¼"–½"), irregularly roundish, lumpy, green maturing to brown; less elongated than those of Northern White Cedar.

Habitat: Wetlands and along stream banks, especially closer to the coast.

Wildlife Use: A preferred food for deer.

EASTERN HEMLOCK (CANADIAN HEMLOCK)
Tsuga canadensis

Look For: *Short, flat, stalked needles about ½" long with 2 white lines on underside; tiny brown cones; thick, dark reddish-brown bark. The widely spaced branches give the tree a delicate, lacy appearance.*

Shape and Form: Medium-sized to large tree with a broadly conical crown and widely spaced branches giving it a "lacy" feel. May be irregularly bushy rather than pointed near the top, and the leading shoot at top may droop.

Bark: Thick, dark reddish-brown to reddish-gray bark with thin, irregular, flat topped ridges. Inner bark, visible in younger trees or when scales are removed, is purplish red. In older trees, scales thicken, become broken by furrows into irregular blocks.

Needles: Stalked needles are short, flat, wider at base and tapering slightly to a rounded tip. (Sides of Fir needles are almost parallel and tip is flat or notched). Needles are about ⅜"–⅝" long, glossy green on top, with 2 white lines on underside. Needles mostly emerge from opposite sides of the twig, about 180⁰ apart, giving the sprays of needles a somewhat flattened appearance. Twig is yellow-brown.

needles - underside

Cones: Numerous, small (⅝"–¾" long), egg-shaped, with thin, flat scales, on outer branches, maturing in fall.

Habitat: Cool, shady sites and north-facing hillsides.

Wildlife Use: Branches and twigs are a favorite winter browse for deer. Large trees are favorite nesting sites for many songbirds and provide winter cover for juncos, warblers, grouse, and deer. Seeds are eaten by pine siskins and chickadees, among others.

Comments: Hemlock is threatened by an aphidlike inset, the Wooly Adelgid.

AMERICAN LARCH (TAMARACK)
Larix laricina

Look For: *Soft, ¾"–1" long, bluish-green needles growing singly or in clusters of ten or more. The only native deciduous conifer: leaves fall off tree in winter.*

Shape and Form: Medium-sized tree, with a straight, tapering trunk and a thin, ovoid or conical crown and irregular, ascending branches.

Bark: Thin, grayish- to reddish-brown, with thin, irregular scales. Twigs are orange-brown.

Needles: Soft, 0.75"–1.0" long, flexible, in clusters of ten or more, at tips of branches and along branches. Needles are light green in spring turning darker in summer, then yellow and falling off in fall. Needles grow singly near ends of new twigs, in clusters of 10–25 near ends of older twigs.

Cones: Small (0.4"–0.8") long, nearly spherical or egg-shaped, upright, with few, thin scales. Reddish at first, ripening to yellowish-brown in fall. May remain attached for several years.

Habitat: Poorly drained bogs, borders of lakes and swamps, or well-drained upland sites, often with other conifers. Intolerant of shade.

Wildlife Use: Not frequently browsed and not widely used for nesting. Finches, yellow throats, and other songbirds may eat seeds.

Comments: The flexible wood of the Larch were used by American Indians to make snowshoes. The thin roots were used to sew together the strips of birch bark used for canoes.

Distinguishing Among the Other Conifers			
Species and Form	**Bark**	**Needles**	**Cones**
Eastern Red Cedar Crown is dense. May be upright and narrowly columnar or spirelike, or broadly conical, or rounded, and bushy. The uppermost shoot may be bent over.	Reddish brown to gray, fibrous, peeling away from the trunk in thin, vertical strips.	Very small (1/16"–3/8") overlapping scales; sprays are not strongly flattened. May also have some small (0.6"), needlelike foliage.	Bluish, berrylike (0.25"–0.40") diameter), with a white, powdery looking, waxy coating, about 1/4" diameter.
Northern White Cedar Compact, pyramidal or broadly conical crown; horizontal branches extending to the ground. Trunk sometimes divided into two secondary trunks.	Thin, fibrous, red-brown to gray-brown, peeling away from the trunk in long, thin, vertical strips.	Made up of tiny (0.3"–0.6"), slightly yellowish-green, overlapping scales on (slightly reddish) brown branchlets in a flattened, fan-shaped array.	Tiny (0.2"–0.4" long), ovoid (somewhat elongated), green turning brown, woody, upright on branches.
Atlantic White Cedar Dense, narrow, pointed, spirelike crown and ascending branches. In mature trees, the crown only begins 3/4 of the way up on the trunk.	Reddish-brown turning ashy-gray, flaky or fibrous, peeling away from the trunk in vertical strips.	Made up of tiny, slightly bluish-green, overlapping scales. On the finest branchlets, the needles form a flattened array, but the several fine branchlets are arrayed in all directions, so overall, the arrays do not appear flattened.	Tiny (.25"–.50" long), green turning brown, roundish but lumpy or irregular.

Distinguishing Among the Other Conifers

Species and Form	Bark	Needles	Cones
Hemlock Broadly conical crown and widely spaced branches, giving tree a "lacey" feel. May be irregularly bushy rather than pointed near the top, and the leading shoot at top may droop.	Thick, dark reddish-brown to reddish-gray bark with thin, irregular, flat topped ridges (thickening into irregular blocks in older trees), yellowish-brown twigs.	Short, flat, blunt tipped, needles about ⅜"–⅝" long, glossy green on top, with 2 white lines on underside. Needles are lined up on two sides of twig, giving the sprays of needles a flattened appearance.	Numerous, 0.6"–0.75" long, egg shaped, with thin, flat scales, on outer branches.
Larch (Tamarack) Straight, tapering trunk and thin, ovoid or conical crown; irregular, ascending branches.	Thin, grayish to reddish brown, with thin, irregular scales and orange-brown twigs.	Soft, 0.75"–1.0" long, flexible, light green in spring turning darker in summer, then yellow and falling in fall. Needles grow singly near ends of new twigs, in clusters of 10–25 on older twigs.	Small, 0.4"–0.8" long, egg-shaped, upright, with few, thin scales.

BROADLEAF TREES

AILANTHUS (TREE OF HEAVEN)
Ailanthus altissima

Look For: *Very large, compound leaves with up to 41 leaflets, each leaflet with teeth only near base. Sometimes shrubby or found in clumps when shaded.*

Shape and Form: Medium-sized tree with single straight trunk, dense crown with ascending branches and very large, pinnately compound leaves. Often forms colonies.

Bark: Light to medium brown and smooth with whitish lenticels in young trees, then darkening and developing shallow fissures with pale furrows visible, and then darkening and becoming rough with interlacing ridges in older trees.

Leaves: Pinnately compound, 6"–30" long with up to 41 leaflets; each leaflet 1"–5" long, elongated ovate to moderately lanceolate; a few large, often rounded teeth near the base.

Seeds: Conspicuous, dense clusters of single-winged samaras (yellowish green turning orange-brown) in late summer/early fall. Ailanthus is a *dioecious* tree (a tree in which the male and female reproductive organs are on different trees). The samaras are found only on the female trees.

Habitat: Widespread, invasive.

Wildlife Use: Not widely used by vertebrate wildlife. Deer browse foliage and mice browse seedlings, but it is not a preferred browse. A few birds eat the seeds. Ants eat the nectar.

Comments: Ailanthus is not native, but because it is able to grow rapidly in the least promising of soils, including in crevices between rocks or paved areas. It has become invasive and widespread. It is the "tree that grew in Brooklyn," a symbol of adaptability and endurance.

young tree   older tree   samaras

buds | flowers, attached to bract | Fruit remnants, attached to bract

Flower: Small clusters of yellowish-white flowers. The stem is attached for part of its length to a leaflike "bract," about three or four times longer than wide.

Fruit: Small (0.25"), round, thick-shelled, gray nut ("monkey nuts"), still attached to the leaflike bract, maturing in fall, and remaining on tree until well after leaves have fallen.

Buds: Greenish or reddish buds on a green or red twig.

Habitat: Moist, rich soils, usually on slopes; shade tolerant.

Wildlife Use: Basswood flowers are a major source of nectar for bees (one of its common names is "Bee Tree"). An acre of Basswoods can produce 800 to 1000 pounds of honey. The leaves are the most preferred food of porcupines from midsummer on.

Comments: The wood has a fine, uniform texture and is prized for hand carving and musical instruments.

AMERICAN BEECH
Fagus grandifolia

Look For: *Smooth, grayish bark, coarsely toothed ovate leaves with an elongated tip; retains dried leaves and has torpedo shaped buds in winter.*

Shape and Form: A large tree with a short trunk and ascending branches and a broad, rounded crown with long, spreading branches.

Bark: Smooth, bluish to ashy gray. With age, splits and becomes darker.

Leaves: Coarsely toothed, ovate with elongated tip, 2"–5" long, shiny dark green. Beeches are early to leave out in spring and may retain some of their dried, straw-colored leaves through much of the winter.

Twigs: Buds in winter are very long (0.4"–0.8"), "torpedo" shaped.

bud   nuts

Nuts: Pairs of small, triangular nuts in a soft-spined, 4 lobed woody husks.
Habitat: Moist, well drained sites. Very shade tolerant.
Wildlife Use: Beech nuts, with their high oil content, are an important winter food for deer, bear, wild turkeys, foxes, squirrels, porcupines, chipmunks, and other small rodents. Beech bark is one of the most important foods for beavers. The leaves are unattractive to most browsers but are eaten by porcupines in the spring. Beeches are very cavity prone and provide shelter for squirrels, wood ducks, barred owls, and other cavity nesters.

The number of nuts a beech tree produces varies widely from year to year. Several other species, including hickories, maples, pines, spruces, and oaks show a similar pattern, which is described in more detail under "oaks" (p. 126).

BIRCHES
Genus Betula
Birches are small to medium-sized trees, often with several trunks and thin, distinctive bark. The flowers take the form of "catkins"—slim, cylindrical flower clusters, with no conspicuous petals, green in spring and summer turning dried and brown—which are retained through the winter.

The bark, leaves, seeds, twigs, and sap provide food for deer, porcupines, ruffed grouse, pine siskins, finches, wood ducks, blue herons, chickadees, and many other songbirds. Birds and squirrels eat the catkins in winter. Older trees are favored for nesting by crows and raptors. Birches are host plants for many species of butterflies and moths, whose caterpillars eat the foliage.

Birches have been widely used by humans, too. Native Americans used the light, flexible, easy-to-strip bark for canoes, bowls, and wigwams, and made syrup from the sap. Oil of wintergreen, from black birches and yellow birches, is used in medicines, as a flavoring (e.g., birch beer, root beer), and in soaps and shampoos. Birch wood is easy to cut and drill, sands to a smooth finish, and stains to produce a uniform finish. As a result, it is a favored wood for toys and high-end furniture. Its physical properties also make it desirable for musical instruments and speaker enclosures.

BLACK BIRCH (SWEET BIRCH)
Betula lenta
Look For: *Smooth dark brown to dark gray bark with horizontal lenticels, sharply toothed leaves with abruptly pointed tip, wintergreen odor to scraped twigs.*

Shape and Form: A medium-sized tree with rounded crown and spreading branches.

Bark: Smooth with horizontal lenticels; reddish-brown when young (similar to young Black Cherry) turning dark grayish. The bark does not peel away from the trunk, except occasionally in older trees.

Leaves: Elongated ovate, with sharp, fine teeth or double teeth, a fine,

pointed tip, and sometimes a heart-shaped base. May be asymmetric.

Flowers: Multiple male catkins, 1.0"–1.6" long, dangling near tip of twig; female catkins 0.8"–1.0" long, erect, on twig further from tip. Dried catkins are retained through the winter.

Twigs: Broken or scratched twigs smell like wintergreen.

Habitat: Rich, well drained sites and moderate to dry soil. Shade intolerant. Often grows out of crevices in rocky areas.

GRAY BIRCH
Betula populifolia
Look For: *Pale grayish bark, with dark triangles or chevrons and many short thin, horizontal lenticels; leaves triangular and coarsely doubled toothed.*

Shape and Form: A small tree, low-branched, usually with several curving or leaning trunks and an open, narrow crown. May form clumps or be bushy.

Bark: Chalky white or grayish-white, marked by thin short, horizontal lenticels and rough, dark triangles or chevrons. The bark does not peel away from the trunk.
Flowers: One to two catkins at tips of twigs; no notable smell.
Leaves: Triangular with a flattened or wedge-shaped base, the tip a longish point, double toothed; often

smaller than other birches. The leaf stalk is long and leaves may flutter in wind like those of aspens.
Flowers: Usually solitary male catkins, about 0.75"–1.0" long, hanging all along the twigs; erect female catkin 0.2"–0.3" long on same twigs. Solitary male catkins (sometimes 2) and the shorter, plumper female catkins are retained into winter near the tips of twigs.
Twigs: Unlike black birch and yellow birch, broken twigs do *not* smell like wintergreen.
Habitat: Adaptable. Not shade tolerant.

PAPER BIRCH (WHITE BIRCH)
Betula papyrifera
Look For: *Chalky-white bark, peeling in thin, horizontal strips, with black branch scars and numerous horizontal black lenticels; double-toothed leaves with a short, tapered tip.*
Shape and Form: Usually single trunked, with horizontal or drooping branches and a narrow, open crown. Sometimes a shrub.
Bark: Thin, creamy or chalky whitish bark,

sometimes with pinkish tinge and numerous dark, horizontal lenticels, peeling into papery horizontal strips; black upside-down V-shaped scars on bark.
Leaves: 0.3"–0.4", ovate, double toothed (two sizes of teeth), with pointed tip and rounded base. Underside of leaf a pale green.
Flowers: Multiple elongated catkins, 0.3"–0.4" long, hanging near twig tip; female catkin 1"–1.5" long, erect, further back along twigs. Dried catkins are retained into winter.
Twigs: Unlike black birch and yellow birch, broken twigs do *not* smell like wintergreen.
Habitat: Adaptable. Shade tolerant.

RIVER BIRCH (RED BIRCH)
Betula nigra

Look For: *Peeling, curly bark, coarsely double toothed triangular leaves, and usually a wetland habitat.*

Shape and Form: A small to medium-sized tree, often with leaning or multiple trunks, low branches spreading upwards in a "vase" shape, and an irregular, spreading crown.

Bark: On young trees, variegated silvery-gray, salmon pink, and orangish- or reddish-brown, peeling in thin, ragged sheets. Older trees more reddish brown and dark gray, with less peeling.

Leaves: Small (1.5"–3" long), triangular to ovate with pointed tip, coarsely double toothed or slightly lobed; shiny dark green with whitish, hairy underside.

Flowers: 3–4 catkins, 1"–2.5" long, near tip of twigs; 0.4" long female catkin erect, shaggy, further back along twigs on a short stem. Catkins ripen earlier than on other birches and persist into winter.

Habitat: Stream and river banks, wetlands, flood plains where seasonally inundated.

YELLOW BIRCH
Betula alleghaniensis

Look For: *Yellowish, peeling bark, coarsely double-toothed leaves, wintergreen odor to scraped twigs.*

Shape and Form: A medium-sized to large tree with a narrow, rounded crown and drooping branches.

Bark: Thin, smooth yellowish-bronze to silvery-gray bark, peeling from ends in horizontal strips. Becomes darker with wide, brown, yellow, or creamy plates in older trees.

Leaves: Ovate, coarsely double toothed (two sizes of teeth), widest near base. May be asymmetric.

Twigs: Broken or scratched twigs smell like wintergreen.

Flowers: 3–4 male catkins, 1"–3" long, dangling near end of twigs; female catkin erect, further back on twig, 0.6"–0.8" long. Dried catkins retained into winter.

Habitat: Prefers cool, moist sites, pond and stream banks, swamps.

Distinguishing Among the Birches

	Bark	Leaf	Twigs	Habitat
Black Birch (Sweet Birch)	Reddish-brown with horizontal lenticels when young, turning dark grayish; bark does not peel except in old trees.	Elongated ovate, with a rounded or heart-shaped base; finely toothed or double toothed margins.	Broken or scratched twigs smell like wintergreen.	Moist, well-drained sites; not shade tolerant.
Gray Birch	Chalky white or grayish-white, with thin short, horizontal lenticels and rough, dark triangles or chevrons. Bark does not peel.	Triangular with a rounded or flattened base; longish pointed tip; double toothed margins.	Broken or scratched twigs do not smell like wintergreen.	Moist or well-drained forests; old fields and pastures; not shade tolerant.
Paper Birch (White Birch)	Creamy white or chalky; dark inverted "v"-shaped scars; peeling in horizontal strips.	Rounded base; double toothed margins.	Broken or scratched twigs do not smell like wintergreen.	Tolerant of wide range of habitats; often in open woods and wood edges; shade tolerant.
River Birch (Red Birch)	On young trees, variegated silvery gray, salmon pink, and orangish or reddish brown, peeling in thin, ragged sheets. Older trees more reddish brown and dark gray, with less peeling.	Triangular to ovate, coarsely double toothed or slightly lobed; shiny dark green with whitish, hairy underside.	Broken or scratched twigs do not have a strong wintergreen odor.	Stream and river banks, wetlands, flood plains where seasonally inundated.
Yellow Birch	Yellowish-bronze to silvery-gray; peeling in horizontal strips.	Rounded base; coarsely double toothed margins.	Broken or scratched twigs smell like wintergreen.	Moist soils, stream and pond banks, wetlands; shade tolerant.

BUTTERNUT (WHITE WALNUT)
Juglans cinereal

Look For: *Long, alternately arranged, pinnately compound leaves with numerous elongated leaflets and large (2") fruits with a sticky husk.*

Shape and Form: A small to medium-sized tree, sometimes with a short or crooked trunk, and an open, somewhat flat-topped crown.

Bark: Light gray or brownish, smooth when young, becoming deeply furrowed. Twigs may be sticky.

Leaves: Pinnately compound, 16"–24" long, with 8–23 leaflets, each leaflet 2"–4.5" long, elongated ovate to broadly lanceolate, pointed at tip and unevenly rounded at base, finely toothed. Terminal leaflet may be missing. Leaflets are "sessile" (attached to midrib with no stem). Axis of young leaves is sticky.

Seeds: Clusters of 3–5 elongated egg-shaped nuts, each 1.5"–2.5" long, tapering at tip. The greenish husk is sticky to the touch.

Habitat: Adaptable in upland sites. Most common in rich, moist soil, but also seen in rocky sites.

Wildlife Use: The nuts are edible for humans and are eaten by blue jays and by squirrels and other small mammals, as well as larger species.

Comments: Before the Civil War, the husks and bark were used to make a yellow-brown dye. Southern migrants to the North wore homespun clothes dyed with the stain, leading to "butternut" becoming a slang term for Southerners. Later, during the Civil War, many Confederate soldiers also wore uniforms dyed with butternut dye or wore gray uniforms that had faded to a brown color much like butternut and were also often referred to as "butternuts."

Butternut and Black Walnut (p. 152) are very similar. The twigs of Butternut are covered with sticky hairs, unlike Black Walnut. The underside of Butternut leaflets is densely covered with hairs, which are inconspicuous in Black

Walnut. The fruits of Butternut are slightly elongated and come to a blunt point, while those of Black Walnut are round. The husk of Butternuts is sticky unlike that of Black Walnuts. The three-lobed leaf scars of Butternut have small dense hairs extending crosswise along the upper margin. They have been described as looking like "monkey faces." The leaf scars of Black Walnut are distinctly notched along the top, with hairs, if any, only in the notch.

NORTHERN CATALPA
Catalpa speciose

Look For: *Medium-sized tree with spreading branches, large heart shaped leaves, conspicuous flowers in spring, and clusters of long, beanlike pods in fall.*

Shape and Form: Medium sized tree with trunk tapering from thick base, spreading branches, and a narrow, rounded crown.

Bark: Brownish-gray, fissured, thin, loose scales.

Leaves: May be opposite or whorled (3 at a node). Large (4"–12" long, 4"–8" wide), thick, with a long (0.4"–0.6") stalk, rounded or heart-shaped base, and a pointed tip. Most leaves are ovate, but some deeply indented. In winter, leaf scars are sunken, resembling suction cups, and the whorled arrangement (3 scars per node) is easily seen.

Flowers: Very large (2"–2.25"), white, bell-shaped flowers with yellow and purple spots, in clusters in late spring.

Fruit: Long (8"–20"), slender, beanlike pods; green turning dark brown, persisting through the winter.

Habitat: Moist soils by streams and riverbanks and swamp margins, but widely naturalized to open areas and roadsides.

Comment: Distinguish from the non-native but often naturalized Southern Catalpa (*C. bignonioides*) by the latter's larger leaves, which smell unpleasant when crushed.

BLACK CHERRY
Prunus serotine

Look For: *A medium- to large-sized tree with very dark scaly bark, looking as if the tree is covered in black cornflakes. Leaves are elongated ovals; small dark fruit in fall.*

Shape and Form: A medium- to large-sized tree, with a short trunk, and an oblong crown.

Bark: Young trees have reddish brown bark with horizontal lenticels (much like Black Birch). In older trees, the bark has very dark scales, often described as "cornflake-like" or "potato chip-like." Red/brown under-bark may show through. Broken twigs have bitter almond smell.

Leaves: 2"–5" long, elongated ovate (length 1.5–3 times width), pointed, with fine teeth. Dark lustrous green on top, paler below.

Flowers: Drooping 0.2"–0.4" long white flowers, forming showy 4"–6" long clusters, after leaves appear.

Fruit: Round, 0.3"–0.4" diameter, red when young, lustrous purplish black when ripe, with large pit.

Habitat: Prefers rich, moist, well-drained soils, but adaptable.

Wildlife Use: The fruits are an excellent late-summer food for opossums, raccoons, bear, foxes, small rodents, and by crows, eastern kingbirds, northern flickers, yellow bellied sapsuckers, blue jays, catbirds, robins and other thrushes, and many other songbirds. The bark is eaten by porcupines, mice, and voles, and the leaves are browsed by deer.

PIN CHERRY
Prunus pennsylvanica

Look For: *A shrub or small, slender tree (rarely more than 25 feet tall) with shiny red twigs.*

Shape and Form: A shrub or small, slender tree with horizontal branches and an open, rounded crown.

Bark: Young trees have smooth, reddish-brown bark with numerous horizontal

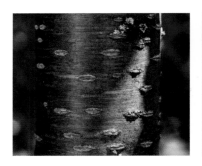

lenticels, becoming gray and fissured, with scaly plates; horizontal lenticels remain evident.

Leaves: 0.25"–0.50", thick, elongated dark green ovals (length about 3 times width), with a long, pointed tip, fine teeth. Leaves are longer than Black Cherry.

Flowers: Clusters of 3–7 small (0.4") flowers.

Fruit: Round, 0.25" diameter, red when young, lustrous purplish-black when ripe, with large pit.

Habitat: Prefers rich, moist, well-drained soils, but adaptable, common on roadsides and in recently disturbed ground.

Wildlife Use: The fruits are an excellent summer food for songbirds such as thrushes, grosbeaks, and waxwings, and mammals, including squirrels, deer, and bear. The leaves are browsed by deer.

AMERICAN CHESTNUT
Castanea dentata

Look For: *A sapling, with long, thin, coarsely toothed and bristle-tipped leaves and a sharp tip.*

At one time, chestnuts comprised 25 percent of all the trees in northeastern hardwood forests. Today they are rare, all but wiped out by the Chestnut Blight, a fungal disease. Between 1900 and 1950, 99.9 percent of American

chestnuts died. Sprouts still arise from the stumps, but the sprouts remain susceptible to the blight. The sprouts grow to sapling size, then die off.

Shape and Form: Full-grown chestnuts were very large, majestic trees, but the remaining chestnuts are almost invariably saplings, sometimes multi-stemmed.

Bark: Smooth, brown, with irregularly vertical tan stripes.

Leaves: 4"–6" long, thin (almost papery), obovate or elongated ovals (length up to 3 times width), with sharp tip. Edges are coarsely toothed with bristles on teeth, giving a saw-tooth appearance. Top dark green, bottom paler. Leaves along the twig may vary in size.

Fruit: Spiny burr, 0.25"–0.3" diameter, enclosing 1–3 nuts.

Habitat: Well drained, upland sites.

COTTONWOOD
Populus deltoides

Look For: *A large tree, with a massive trunk, deeply furrowed bark, spreading branches, and triangular to heart shaped leaves, growing in or near wetlands and near ponds and streams.*

Shape and Form: A large tree, often with a massive trunk, spreading, slightly drooping branches, and an irregular, open crown. The trunk may fork low down.

Bark: Very thick, brown to brownish gray, with shallow, reddish furrows and ridges broken horizontally into variably shaped blocks. In older trees, furrows deepen; the reddish furrows are obscured and ridges form often dramatically rugged, irregular blocks.

Leaves: More or less triangular, less than 6" long, with a flattened or heart-shaped base, somewhat elongated tip, and rounded, blunt teeth. The long-stemmed leaves flutter in even light breezes.

Flowers and Fruit: Male and female flowers grow on separate trees. The male flower is a 3"–4" long gold, reddish (turning green) catkin. The yellowish-green female flower is 2"–3" cm long. When they mature, the fruit capsules open, releasing small seeds attached to fluffy cottonlike strands (giving the tree its name).

Habitat: Rich, moist sites, most commonly bordering ponds, streams, wet fields. Shade tolerant.

Wildlife Use: Cottonwood is not especially valuable as food, though beavers eat the bark and deer occasionally browse twigs and leaves. The branches break easily in the wind, leaving nesting sites for cavity nesters.

DOGWOOD
Cornus florida

Look For: *A small, understory tree with oppositely arranged leaves and bark with small, regularly arranged plates. In spring, showy white (or less commonly, pink) "flowers," in winter, globular terminal buds, flattened on the bottom with a slight point at the top.*

Shape and Form: A small tree with a short trunk, a rounded crown, and relatively sparse foliage.

Bark: Grayish to black with small, regularly arranged, scaly plates evident even on very young trees.

Leaves: Oppositely arranged, ovate, with smooth edges, abrupt tip. Veins curve up towards tip rather than running to edge of leaf.

Flower: What is usually thought of as the dogwood "flower" is really four large (1"–2" long) white or pinkish "bracts" (modified leaves), widest above the middle and notched at the top. These surround the actual flower, which is a very small, yellowish, headlike cluster.

Fruit: Clusters of bright red, ⅓"–½" long berries, in late summer or fall

Habitat: An understory tree. Shade tolerant. Commonly cultivated.

Wildlife Use: The fruits are eaten by deer, rabbits, squirrels, skunks, and foxes, as well as by wild turkeys, woodpeckers, and a wide variety of fruit-eating songbirds.

bud

flowers

berries

AMERICAN ELM
Ulmus americana

Look For: *A straight trunk with narrow buttresses at the base; coarsely double-toothed asymmetric leaves, oval samaras in spring to early summer.*

At one time, elms were very common and were used widely as ornamental trees in parks. Since the 1930s, however, a fungus spread by Elm Bark Beetles has destroyed most elms.

Shape and Form: A large tree with a straight trunk, often with narrow, flange-like buttresses at the base, and ascending branches forming a spreading, "vase-shaped" crown.

Bark: Young trees have soft and spongy grayish-brown bark, with vertical strips or scales. Mature trees may have persisting long vertical ridges, intersecting to form diamond-shaped furrows, or may be scaly, with narrow ridges and furrows.

Leaves: 3"–6" long, 1"–3" wide, smooth to slightly rough, coarsely double-toothed; obovate, ovate, or elliptic; with very prominent, parallel veins, a moderately or strongly asymmetric base and an abrupt point.

Flowers: Small drooping clusters of 3–5 small, reddish-green flowers on short stalks, in early spring before the leaves appear.

Fruit: The flattened seed is covered by an oval, thin, paperlike samara, 0.3"–0.4" wide, with hairs on the edges and a deep notch at the base. Samaras appear in mid-Spring.

Habitat: A bottomland tree, preferring rich, moist soils and margins of wetlands, but will grow elsewhere, as well.

Wildlife Use: More than 500 species of insect breed, food, or take shelter in elms. The early-appearing buds and flowers and the seeds are an important spring food for squirrels, foxes, and opossums. Deer and woodchucks browse foliage and young twigs. Elms also provide good cover for nesting songbirds.

samara

SLIPPERY ELM
Ulmus rubra

Look For: *A straight high branching trunk with coarsely double-toothed asymmetric leaves that are rough to the touch; oval samaras in spring to early summer.*

Shape and Form: Medium-sized tree, with an open, flat-topped crown. The trunk is usually free of branches for a greater length than American elm and the branches less arched.

Bark: Similar to American Elm. Gray to dark reddish brown, somewhat spongy when young, with broad vertical strips that may separate from trunk on one edge. Inner bark on trunk and twigs is mucilaginous, tastes like licorice.

Leaves: Ovate to elliptical, 4"–6" long, long pointed; edges coarsely and sharply double toothed; with prominent, parallel veins; base asymmetric; upper surface very rough, lower surface less rough and somewhat hairy.

Seeds: Nearly round, light green, papery samara, 0.5"–1" across, in late spring. Unlike American Elm, the samaras are not notched and have hairless margins,

Habitat: Moist soils

Comment: The leaves of American Elm and the two other elm species found in Connecticut, Slippery Elm (*U. rubra*) and the non-native Wych Elm (*U. glabra*) have a similar shape but Slippery Elm and Wych Elm both have leaves that feel very rough to the touch on their upper surface, and the Wych Elm leaves are conspicuously toothed.

samara

WYCH ELM
Ulmus glabra

Wych Elm was introduced from Europe. It has become established along roadsides and woodland margins in the US (The name "wych" has nothing to do with witches. It comes from an Old English word meaning "pliant"). The leaves and bark are much like Slippery Elm. Leaves have hairs on both sides. The samara is slightly notched, hairless on the margins.

Distinguishing Among the Elms

	Leaves	Samaras
American Elm	Smooth or slightly rough to the touch. Tufts of hairs in vein axils.	Deeply notched. Hairy on margins, sparsely hairy on surface.
Slippery Elm	Very rough to the touch.	Not notched. Hairless on margins, hairless on surface.
Wych Elm	Very rough to the touch; may have 3 lobelike points at upper end.	Slightly notched. Hairless on margins, hairs only on midvein.

COMMON HACKBERRY
Celtis occidentalis

Look For: *A medium- to large-sized tree with asymmetric leaves that are smooth near the base but conspicuously toothed further up on the leaf; gray, warty bark; and a low-branching, broad, rounded crown.*

Shape and Form: A medium-sized tree, with a trunk that is unbranched for most of its length and a broad crown.

Bark: In young trees smooth and light brown or gray, developing wartlike protuberances along the trunk, which grow together to create ridges in older trees.

Leaves: Thin, ovate, about 3"–5" long and about twice as long as broad, with an elongated point and a usually strongly asymmetric base. Edges are smooth near the base but conspicuously toothed further up on the leaf. The twigs are thin and may curve back towards their base.

Fruits: Small (¼"–⅜"), round, orange-red turning to dark purple in the early fall. Dried, wrinkled fruits often remain on the tree well into winter.

Habitat: Prefers moist, well-drained soils, stream banks, but adaptable to many soil types.

Wildlife Use: The berries are eaten by many birds and small and mid-sized mammals but are not a preferred food source, probably because the seed is large and the pulp thin.

Comment: "Witches brooms"—dense clusters of twigs, often growing from a single point, and resembling a broom, caused by mites or fungi—are often found in Hackberry trees and may be nesting sites for songbirds.

HAWTHORNS
Genus Crataegus
Look For: *Shrub or small tree with one or more trunks; long thorns on branches and twigs, usually sharply toothed or lobed leaves.*

Most Hawthorns are shrubs, but some species may take the form of a small tree, less than 35' (and usually less than 20') tall. There are several hundred named species of Hawthorn in the US, including several dozen in Connecticut. Distinguishing the particular species that make up the genus *Crataegus* is often problematic, even for experts. Distinctions are more reliable among several "sections" within the genus and among "series" within each section. To complicate identification further, the various species hybridize extensively. Hawthorns are common on the edges of woods and fields, in pastures and abandoned fields, and on stream banks. Although the fruits are eaten by birds and mammals, the most important wildlife value of hawthorns is as cover.

Hawthorns as a group are easy to identify by the large (often longer than 1") thorns on their branches and twigs (and sometimes on the trunk, as well); showy clusters of ½"–1" white or pink flowers at the ends of twigs in spring;

Distinguishing Among the Hickories

	Leaves	Bark	Twigs and Terminal Buds	Nut
Shagbark	5 (3–7) leaflets, top three larger than others.	Light to dark gray; vertically striped in young trees; very shaggy in mature trees with ends of long, loose, flat plates often well separated from trunk.	Bud: Large (⅓"–⅔"), brown, overlapping scales, hairy. Twig: Stout, brown, or reddish brown, hairy or hairless	Round; thick husk, 1.0"–2.0" diameter; shell splits into 4 sections at base.
Pignut	5–9 (usually 5 or 7) leaflets, usually tending to be of fairly uniform size. Petiole not hairy.	Smooth or with shallow furrows and interlacing ridges and short, horizontal cuts. Ridges are sometimes shaggy-topped.	Bud: Small (less than ⅔"), light brown, overlapping scales. Twig: Relatively slender with tan-colored lenticels, smooth or a few hairs, brown or reddish brown.	Oval or pear shaped, often with a "snoutlike" protrusion at the base; thin husk that does not split away. 1"–2" long. Shell has strong lemon smell when scratched.
Mockernut	5–9 (average 7) leaflets, top leaflets larger and lowest pair smaller than others; underside of leaves and petioles covered with short hairs. Hairy, especially along veins.	Gray, with lighter gray ridges and darker diamondlike furrows. Furrows deeper than other hickories.	Bud: Large (about ⅖"–⅗"), light brown overlapping scales, hairy (may be silvery). Twig: Stout, light brown to reddish or grayish brown, hairy, especially towards ends.	Round or ovate; thick husk, 1.5"–2" diameter.
Bitternut (Sulfur-yellow terminal buds)	7–11 (usually 9) relatively small, usually elongated leaflets, with top three bigger than others. Hairy petiole.	Smooth or with shallow vertical furrows and interlacing ridges.	Bud: Long, yellowish, slightly flattened, with two opposing scales, a few hairs. Twig: Thin, hairless, grayish or greenish brown with tan lenticels.	Round; thin husk, slightly ridged or "winged" and often a point at stem end, 0.75"–1.25" diameterHusk splits away at base when mature.

AMERICAN HOLLY
Ilex opaca
Look For: *Shrub or small evergreen tree with stiff, spiny leaves. The familiar holly of Christmas decorations*
Shape and Form: A shrub or small tree, with a pyramidal crown with branches close to the ground, or with an irregular or somewhat conical crown.
Bark: Smooth, gray with darker areas.
Leaves: Evergreen. Stiff, curled, elliptical, 3" long, dark glossy green above, pale green underleaf, with several sharp spines at the edges.
Fruit: ¼" red berries in small clusters, on female trees only.
Habitat: Understory in open woods; prefers moist soils but can be found in dry, sandy soils
Wildlife Use: The berries provide food for many birds and mammals. Used as cover by songbirds.

EASTERN HOPHORNBEAM
Ostrya virginiana
Look For: *Very shaggy, reddish-brown to grayish-brown bark; oppositely branching, elongated simple, ovate leaves*
Shape and Form: A small- to medium-sized tree, usually less than 40' tall, with a broad, pyramidal crown becoming rounded with age.
Bark: Younger tree has reddish-brown to grayish-brown bark, divided into narrow, shaggy, vertically rectangular strips, loose on ends. In older trees, strips thicken but remain detached at ends.
Leaves: Elongated ovate, 3"–5" long, irregularly double toothed with slender tip and rounded or heart-shaped base. Top and bottom surface is lightly hairy. May retain many dried leaves into winter.
Flowers: Catkins, appearing with the leaves, usually in hanging clusters of three at the end of twigs, retained into the winter.
Habitat: Dry, rich soils, most often on slopes or ridges. Very shade tolerant.

Wildlife Use: Rabbits, deer, wild turkeys, ruffed grouse, downy woodpeckers, rose-breasted grosbeaks, and purple finches, among others, eat the seeds of Hophornbeam. Because the catkins remain on the tree in the winter, it provides an important winter food source. Small birds and bats nest under the loose strips of bark.

AMERICAN HORNBEAM (BLUE BEECH, MUSCLEWOOD, IRONWOOD)

Carpinus caroliniana

Look For: *A small, shrubby, understory tree with a smooth, gray, fluted or muscular-looking trunk.*

Shape and Form: A small (usually less than 30'), shrubby tree with one or more short, gray, fluted or "muscular" trunks, often angled or twisted; widely spreading branches; and a broad, flat-topped crown

Bark: Very smooth, blue-gray bark, looking "twisted" or "muscular" or "rippled" or "sinewy"

Leaves: Elongated ovate, shiny, double-toothed leaves, with a rounded base and pointed tip, about 4" long.

Flowers: Reddish green catkins (male 1.0"–1.5" long, along twig; female 0.5"–0.75" long, at tip of twig).

Fruit: Samara-like seeds are surrounded by a three-lobed sepal, placed like an umbrella over the seed.

seeds

Habitat: Rich, moist sites, often bordering ponds or streams or wetlands. Very shade tolerant.

Wildlife Use: Hornbeam seeds are eaten by squirrels and other small rodents. Beavers use hornbeam for building dams and lodges.

HORSE CHESTNUT
Aesculus hippocastanum

Look For: *Palmately compound leaves with 5–9 (average 7) leaflets; prickly fruit capsule in fall.*

Shape and Form: A medium-sized to large tree with a broadly conical crown with a rounded top.

Bark: Dark brown, with shallow furrows divided into thin irregular plates.

Leaves: Oppositely arranged, palmately compound leaves, with 5–9 leaflets growing from a common point. Overall leaf about 12"–16" across; each large irregularly and coarsely toothed leaflet is obovate, with short-pointed tip.

Flowers: Showy, 4"–6" by 8"–10" white flowers in spring with leaves.

Fruit: 2" diameter capsule covered with prickles containing one or more ½"–1" seeds.

Habitat: Non-native, but widely cultivated and naturalized. Adaptable but prefers moist, well-drained soil.

Comments: Horse Chestnut is non-native but has widely naturalized. Horse Chestnut nuts ("conkers") contain toxic alkaloids and are not edible. Deer and squirrels are among the few mammals that are able to eat them without harm.

BLACK LOCUST
Robinia pseudoacacia

Look For: *Very deeply furrowed brown to dark grayish-brown bark with complexly intersecting, ropelike ridges; oppositely arranged, pinnately compound leaves with 1"–2" long oval leaflets and small thorns at base of leaves.*

Shape and Form: Medium-sized tree, with straight or crooked trunk and irregular crown of ascending branches.

Bark: In young trees, flat, pale, grayish ridges alternate with broad, shallow, darker, sometimes slightly rust-colored furrows, producing rough vertical stripes. In older trees, the furrows darken and deepen dramatically. The light brown to grayish brown bark becomes very rugged, with very deep furrows and twisting or complexly interlocking ropelike vertical ridges.

Leaves: Pinnately compound, 8"–12" long overall, with 7–25 smooth-edged, egg-shaped 1½" long, blue-green leaflets, usually with a small point at end.

Flowers: Clusters of showy white flowers after leaves open, late spring or early summer.

Fruit: Oblong, flat pod, 2"–4" long, late summer to fall, which may persist into winter. (Black Locust reproduces more vigorously by root suckering and stump sprouting than by its seeds germinating. It forms groves of trees interconnected by a common root system.)

Thorns: Usually a pair of small thorns or spines at base of leaves. Younger trees may have thorns on the trunk, as well. Thorns are variable: Some trees have no thorns at all, while others are densely prickly. Thorns are more common in young trees and branches near the ground.

Habitat: An early succession tree, colonizing disturbed areas. Prefers moist woods, stream margins, old pastures, disturbed roadsides, but can grow in a variety of soils, unless they are excessively dry or are wet and poorly drained. Shade intolerant.

Wildlife Use: The twigs and leaves of Black Locust are toxic, so they are not widely used for food. Black Locust flowers are a major source of nectar for bees. An acre of Black Locusts can produce 800 to 1200 pounds of honey.

Comments: Black Locust is native as far north as Pennsylvania. In Connecticut, it is often seen as invasive. Its root sprout colonies may choke out native vegetation. Black Locust is a legume, and like other legumes, it can fix nitrogen, enriching the soil. In coastal areas, where the soil may have low nutrient value, this may increase the available nitrogen, threatening native species that are adapted to nitrogen-poor soils. However, Black Locust, unlike many

thorns   seed pods

so-called invasive species, does host a number of insect species—in fact, a larger number than native trees such as Sassafras, Sycamore, and Eastern White Cedar.

MAPLES
Genus Acer

Maples are unusual in their reproductive character. Some species of maple are *monoecious* (i.e., have both male and female flowers on each tree), but Boxelders are *dioecious* (i.e., some trees are male, others female). Red Maple and Striped Maple are "*polygamodioecious.*" Some individual trees have male flowers, others have female flowers, and some have both male and female flowers. Some trees can completely switch genders, showing all male flowers some years, all female in other years, and a mixture of genders in other years.

The number of samaras a maple produces vary widely from year to year. Many other species, including hickories, beeches, pines, spruces, and oaks show a similar pattern, which is described in more detail under "Oaks" (p. 126).

BLACK MAPLE
Acer nigrum

Look For: *A large tree with oppositely arranged, lobed (usually 3 lobes; sometimes 5) leaves. Leaves may droop on each side, as if the tree needs watering. Samaras with wings spread less than 60°, appear in fall.*

Shape and Form: A large tree with a short trunk and broad, dense, oval crown.

Bark: Like Sugar Maple, but more deeply divided by furrows, and plates may be more regular.

Leaves: 3 lobes (sometimes 5). The terminal (center) lobe is wider at the base than near the tip and the sinuses between the lobes tend to be broadly "U"-shaped. The undersides of the leaves and the petioles (leaf stems) are covered with fine hairs. The tips of lobes may droop, as if the tree needs water. The terminal lobe has few if any teeth. Leaves are relatively thick.

Flowers: Yellow, dangling in clusters, appearing with the leaves.

Twigs and buds: Terminal buds are small, brown, pointed, covered with hairs. Lenticels on the branchlets are relatively large and prominent compared to those of Sugar Maple.

Seeds: 1" long samara, "U"-shaped or with wings spread less than 60°, maturing in early autumn

Comments: Habitat overlaps with Sugar Maple but more likely than Sugar Maple to be found in wet soil. Sugar Maple and Black Maple are very similar and may be hard to distinguish. Some experts consider Black Maple to be a subspecies of Sugar Maple. They often hybridize, producing trees whose characteristics are intermediate between those of the parent trees. Along with Sugar Maple, Black Maple is used for commercial maple sugar production.

BOXELDER
Acer negundo

Look For: *The combination of oppositely arranged compound leaves with three to five smooth edged leaflets (sometimes ovate, sometimes shallowly or deeply lobed), multiple trunks, two-winged samaras, and twigs that are green or purplish or bluish. (Distinguish from Ashes, which usually have more than three leaflets, single-winged samaras, and twigs that are gray or brown).*

Shape and Form: Medium-sized tree, usually low and spreading with multiple, leaning trunks or with a single trunk divided near the ground, and a broad irregularly rounded crown.

Bark: Smooth, grayish or brownish when young; darkening, with scaly ridges in mature trees

Twigs: Greenish or bluish or purplish.

Leaves: Opposite, compound leaves, 4"–6" overall, with 3–5 leaflets. (The leaves may look like poison ivy, but Boxelder is a tree, not a vine). Leaflet shape is variable—from ovate with pointed tip to shallowly or deeply lobed. End leaflet has longer stem and sharply pointed tip. Edges are smooth or a have few coarse teeth.

Flowers: Drooping clusters of pale greenish-yellow or reddish flowers appear in early spring, before the leaves appear.

Seeds: Boxelder is dioecious: Male and female flowers are found on different trees. Clusters of two-winged "V"-shaped samaras are found on female trees only in late summer or early fall, often persisting through the winter.

Habitat: Stream banks, edges of swamps, flood plains.

Comment: The only maple with compound leaves.

MOUNTAIN MAPLE

Acer spicatum

Mountain Maple is usually a shrub, with multiple trunks and many stems extending from near the base. Occasionally it takes the form of a small tree, rarely attaining a height greater than 20–25 feet. The bark is thin, brown, smooth in young trees, then becoming scaly. The leaves are 2"–4" across with three or sometimes five shallow lobes and coarse teeth. The wings of the samara are 0.75"–1.0" long.

Mountain Maple grows best in moist, well-drained soil and thrives along stream and riverbanks, where it stabilizes the soil.

NORWAY MAPLE

Acer platanoides

Look For: *Relatively large, opposite, lobed leaves and usually 5 lobes with points at ends of lobes (much like Sugar Maple); stems and leaf veins exude a milky sap if broken.*

Norway Maple looks a lot like Sugar Maple. Unlike Sugar Maple, however, a milky sap is exuded from its reddish leaf stems and leaf veins if they are broken or cut. The leaves are a little wider than long, unlike Sugar Maple leaves, which are usually longer than wide. Norway Maples hold their green leaves later than almost any other Connecticut tree. A tree that is still green in early November is likely to be a Norway Maple.

Norway Maple is not a native tree and is often invasive. It is very fertile and grows vigorously in a wide variety of soils. It shades out other plants and is itself easily grown in shade. It is relatively resistant to insects and fungi that affect other maples. As a result, it has been supplanting sugar maples, oaks, and other native trees in many areas. It is of much less value to wildlife than oaks, so its spread is associated with a decline in the variety and numbers of bird species.

RED MAPLE
Acer rubrum

Look For: *Smallish (less than 4"), coarsely toothed leaves with three (sometimes 5) lobes and reddish stems; reddish flowers before leaves appear; small, often reddish samara maturing in spring.*

Shape and Form: A medium-sized to large tree with stocky branches. Young trees have a pyramidal crown, which becomes broader and rounder as the tree matures.

Leaves: 3 lobes (occasionally 5), smaller than Sugar Maple leaves, with narrow, sharp pointed tips, a flattish bottom, relatively narrow sinuses between lobes, and roughly toothed edges. The terminal lobe is wider at the base than near the tip. Underside of leaves is whitened. The leaf stalk is red.

Bark: Smooth, grayish-brown bark of young tree darkens and cracks deepen as tree ages. Bark of older tree is grayish-brown with vertical cracks, forming long, vertical, narrow, platelike strips. The strips may detach and curl outward at one or both ends but remain attached. The bark is often infected by "target canker," a fungus that causes the bark to crack in concentric circles.

target canker

Twigs and buds: The leaf stalk and twigs are often reddish, with a large, rounded, sometimes reddish terminal bud.

Flower: Small, reddish (female) or yellow-orange (male) flowers in early spring, appearing before leaves.

Seeds: 1" long wings spread less than 60°; often red, maturing in late spring, hanging from tree in clusters looking almost like flowers.

Habitat: Very adaptable. Very common in wet wooded areas and edges of ponds and streams; more scattered in upland woods.

Wildlife Use: The seeds, buds, and sap feed many insects and provide good summer food and nesting sites. Red Maple twigs and leaves are not a preferred

samara flower samaras on tree

browse for deer. The seeds appear early and are a primary food source for squirrels and chipmunks. Red maples are also a relatively poor tree for nesting, but younger trees may provide nesting sites for robins, goldfinches, purple finches, yellow bellied sapsuckers, American redstarts, and some warblers.

SILVER MAPLE
Acer saccharinum

Look For: *Coarsely toothed leaves with five, almost fingerlike lobes, deep "U"-shaped sinuses, and a terminal lobe narrower at the base than near the tip. The samaras are large (2"), widely winged, mature in late spring to early summer.*

Shape and Form: A medium-sized to large tree with a short, stout trunk, a few large branches beginning low on the trunk, and a broad, irregularly rounded crown.

Bark: Bark of young trees is smooth and silvery-gray, sometimes with a reddish tinge, and vertical cracks. The paler tan to reddish-brown inner bark is visible in the furrows. Bark of older trees is grayish-brown, shaggy, with layers of long, thin, vertical scaly plates. Plates may detach at one or both ends.

Leaves: 5 lobed, with deep U-shaped sinuses, edges sharply toothed, and the terminal lobe narrowest at its base. The leaves are silvery white on the underside (giving the tree its name).

Seeds: Samara about up to 2" wide with widely spread wings, maturing in late spring

Habitat: Rich, moist sites, often bordering water.

Wildlife Use: Similar to Red Maple. Silver Maples are cavity prone and provide nesting sites for owls, raccoons, and others.

STRIPED MAPLE
Acer pennsylvanicum

Look For: *A small tree with leaves with three shallow lobes, a rounded or heart-shaped base, and a reddish stem; bark (especially in younger trees) marked by grayish- or brownish-green and creamy white stripes; samara with very widely spread wings appears in late summer or early fall.*

Shape and Form: A small tree with a short trunk often splitting into several branches near the ground, and ascending or arching branches. Often grows as a shrub, less than 20' tall.

Bark: Young tree (and older branches) are smooth, grayish-green or brownish-green, with narrow vertical, creamy white stripes; mature tree with darker, thicker, warty bark and striped or shallow vertical ridges.

Leaves: 3 lobed (sometimes with 2 additional small lobes at base), with finely double toothed edges and a rounded or heart-shaped base. Leaves may be large (7"–9").

Seeds: Samara is about 1.0"–1.5" wide with widely spread wings (often described as "like a coat hanger"), maturing in late summer or early autumn.

Habitat: A small understory tree in moist woods and often on pond and stream banks.

Wildlife Use: A favored food for deer, who heavily browse leaves in summer and twigs in winter. The seeds provide fall food for squirrels and other small rodents. Striped maples are not a preferred nesting site for most birds.

SUGAR MAPLE
Acer saccharum

Look For: *A medium-sized to large tree, with relatively large, opposite, lobed leaves (usually 5 lobes), with points at ends of lobes; "U"-shaped samara with wings usually spread less than 60° appears in fall.*

Shape and Form: A medium-sized to large tree with a single, stout trunk, large branches starting fairly close to the ground, and a rounded crown.

Leaves: 5 (rarely 3) smooth or sparsely toothed lobes, with pointed tips and narrow "U"-shaped sinuses between lobes. The sides of center lobe are almost parallel; the under surface of the leaves is pale green. Leaves are relatively thin.

Bark: Smooth, gray when young, becoming darker, thicker, with vertical furrows and irregular, fairly wide, long vertical plates. The plates may look shaggy or ropelike.

Twigs and buds: Terminal bud is small, brown, pointed, has few hairs. Lenticels on the branchlets are relatively small compared to Black Maple.

samara

flower

Distinguishing Among the Maples				
	Leaf	**Bark**	**Seeds (Samaras)**	**Habitat**
Sugar Maple	5 lobes (occasionally 3); sides of top lobe almost parallel. Smooth on underside.	Smooth and gray when young, becoming darker with deep vertical furrows and irregular, fairly wide vertical plates.	Mature in fall. "U"- shaped or spread less than 60°.	Fertile, well-drained soil.
Black Maple	3 (sometimes 5) lobes; sides of top lobe wider than base; downy on underside. Few if any teeth on terminal lobe. Leaves may droop at tips of lobes.	Much like Sugar Maple.	Mature in fall. "U"-shaped or spread less than 60°.	Fertile, well-drained soil; tolerates wet soil.
Red Maple	3 lobes (occasionally 5); stem often reddish; edges coarsely toothed.	Grayish-brown with vertical cracks forming vertical, narrow, platelike strips. (May be infested by "target canker," forming concentric circles of cracks).	Matures in late spring. Wings spread less than 60°.	Adaptable. Common in wet sites and scattered in upland woods.

Distinguishing Among the Maples				
Silver Maple	5 deep lobes; terminal lobe narrower at base; silvery white underneath.	Grayish-brown, shaggy, with layers of long, thin, vertical scaly plates.	Mature in late spring. Wings relatively long, widely spread.	Moist sites, often bordering water.
Striped Maple	3 lobed with finely toothed margins and a rounded or heart-shaped base.	Smooth, grayish-green with narrow, vertical, creamy stripes in young trees; stripes become shallow vertical ridges in older trees.	Mature in late summer or early fall. Widely spread wings.	A small understory tree in moist woods and along pond and stream banks.
Norway Maple	Much like sugar maple. Stem often red. Leaf veins and stems exude a milky white sap when scratched.	Vertical ridges broken into rectangular blocks or forming diamond shaped blocks.	Mature late summer to fall. Widely spread wings.	Non-native and sometimes considered to be invasive.
Boxelder	Compound leaf, with 3–5 leaflets of variable shape.	Often multiple trunks, smooth grayish or brownish when young, darkening with scaly ridges when older.	Mature late summer or early fall.	Stream banks, edges of swamps, flood plains.

Seeds: Winged samara varies from U-shaped to less than 90° between 1" long wings; appears in fall.

Flowers: Dangling clusters of small yellow flowers, as leaves are emerging.

Habitat: Prefers fertile, moist, well-drained soil.

Wildlife Use: The wide distribution of Red Maple makes it a pivotal species for wildlife. Sugar maples are a preferred browse for deer. Porcupines eat the inner bark. In spring, squirrels scrape away the outer bark and lick the sap that oozes out. The seeds provide food for squirrels and a wide variety of birds. Sugar maples are a good nesting site for robins, grosbeaks, and goldfinches, and for many cavity nesters. The leaf litter is important for earthworms.

Comments: Sugar Maples are an important timber tree. The wood is hard, heavy, and strong. The sap is sweeter than that of other maples. As a result, Sugar Maple and its close relative Black Maple are the only maples used today for commercial syrup production. The sap flows when nights are below freezing and days warmer than 40°F.

Sugar Maple and Black Maple are very similar and may be hard to distinguish. (Some experts consider them to be a single species). They often hybridize, producing trees with intermediate characteristics.

AMERICAN MOUNTAIN ASH
Sorbus Americana

NORTHERN MOUNTAIN ASH (SNOWY MOUNTAIN ASH)
Sorbus decora

Despite their name, the Mountain Ashes are not related to the ashes. They are usually shrubs, 10'–20' tall, but occasionally they grow as small trees, sometimes with multiple trunks and with a narrow, rounded crown. As a tree, Mountain Ash has smooth, thin, gray to light brown bark. The leaves are pinnately compound, 4"–8" long, with a reddish stem and 9–17 elongated, toothed leaflets, each 2"–4" long. In early summer, they have showy white clusters of flowers, and in late summer or early fall, clusters of small (¼"–½"), red or orange-red, berries. They are most commonly found in moist sites bordering

swamps, rivers, and ponds., or on rocky hillsides. The fruits, leaves, and shoots all provide food for wildlife. In addition to the flowers and berries the gray bark and relatively small leaves distinguish them from the Sumacs.

The two species of Mountain Ash are very similar and may be hard to distinguish. American Mountain Ash has larger leaves (more than 6") with long points at tips, light gray bark, and ¼" diameter berries. Northern Mountain Ash has shorter leaves (4"–6" with short points at tips, dark gray bark, and 0.4"–0.5" diameter berries. The two species hybridize with each other and also hybridize with Serviceberry.

RED MULBERRY
Morus rubra

WHITE MULBERRY
Morus alba

BLACK MULBERRY
Morus nigra

Look For: *Coarsely toothed leaves of various shapes (circular or ovate or lobed) and white or dark blackberry-like fruit.*

Red Mulberry is native to Connecticut. White Mulberry and Black Mulberry were introduced from Asia but have naturalized and have become more common in Connecticut than Red Mulberry. Black and White Mulberry are sometimes considered to be the same species.

Shape and Form: A small- to medium-sized tree with a low branching trunk, broad, rounded crown, and milky sap. May grow as a shrub.

Bark: Dark brown or reddish brown, fissured.

Leaves: Ovate or nearly circular or heart-shaped, with toothed edges and a short point. May be unlobed or may have several lobes. When leaves are broken off, they exude a milky sap. Distinguish: *Red Mulberry* leaves are dark green,

non-lustrous, and rough-to-the-touch. *White Mulberry* leaves are medium green, lustrous, and smooth-to-the-touch. *Black Mulberry* leaves are smooth on their upper surface but hairy underneath.

Fruits: 1"–2" long blackberry-like fruits, white or red or purple, maturing in summer.

Habitat: Moist soils; common near streams; shade tolerant.

Wildlife Use: The fruits are eaten by a wide variety of birds and mammals.

NANNYBERRY
Viburnum lentago

Look For: *A shrub or small tree (usually less than 20 feet tall) in a wetland habitat, with several slender trunks, finely toothed leaves, showy clusters of tiny white flowers in late spring, and small berries (green in summer, turning bluish black) in fall.*

Shape and Form: A shrub or small tree with several slender, crooked trunks, drooping or arched branches, and a rounded crown.

Bark: Dark reddish brown, to brownish black, broken into small plates.

Leaves: Opposite, ovate or nearly round, finely toothed, with tip narrowing abruptly to a point.

bud

flower   berries

Flower: 2"–4" wide clusters of tiny (¼") white flowers in late spring
Fruit: ⅓"–½" bluish-black berries, which may persist into winter.
Habitat: Grows in wetlands or near streams and ponds. Shade tolerant.
Wildlife Use: A host plant to numerous butterflies and moths. The berries are eaten by many birds and mammals.

OAKS
Genus Quercus
Look For: *Oaks have lobed leaves that are longer than they are wide. In fall, their distinctive capped acorns can be found on the tree or under the tree. In winter, oaks are easily distinguished by multiple terminal buds at the ends of twigs.*

Oaks are the trees of the greatest benefit to wildlife in Eastern North America. They support more than 600 species of insects, which in turn, support many bird species. More than 100 species of mammal and birds eat acorns. A wild turkey may eat 220 acorns in a single "meal." The Northern Red Oak provides up to 55 percent of deer's diet in winter.

Animals, like humans, prefer foods that taste good to them. Although White Oak acorns are lower than Red Oak acorns in oils and protein, they are less tannic. Most mammals prefer the sweeter White Oak acorns, but White Oak acorns germinate very quickly, while red oak acorns lie dormant until spring, when they sprout. As a result, the latter are more available as food later in the season. Squirrels tend to eat the White Oak acorns as soon as they find them but store the Red Oak acorns for later in winter.

The number of acorns oak trees produce varies widely from one year to the next. For several years in a row, they produce a steady but moderate number. Then, in a "mast year," all the trees of a particular species (i.e., all Northern Red Oaks, all Eastern White Oaks) in a particular area produce vast quantities of acorns.

While the full explanation of what triggers a mast year remains uncertain, the dramatic year-to-year variation in acorns has benefits for the tree. For one thing, both nut production and overall tree growth require a lot of energy. By reducing the number of acorns produced in any given year, the tree can grow faster than in the years when large numbers of acorns are produced. Producing large numbers of acorns episodically also helps ensure reproduction. Deer, squirrels, and many other mammals eat most of the acorns in any given year, leaving few to sprout. But limiting the number of acorns available also limits the populations of the animal species dependent on the nuts. Then comes a mast year in which there are far more nuts than usual. The nut-eating animals satisfy their hunger before they consume all the nuts, leaving more to grow into new trees. And animals such as squirrels bury a larger proportion of the acorns instead of eating them immediately. More seeds are again left to sprout.

Several other tree species, including beeches, hickories, maples, spruces, and pines, use a similar strategy.

Oaks also provide nesting sites, both in their branches and in cavities. Since many species of oak retain their dried leaves through the winter, they are an important source of cover for over-wintering songbirds and raptors.

Oaks are major timber trees. The wood is strong, heavy, and durable, making the tree itself a symbol of strength and endurance. Oaks play a prominent role in the mythologies of peoples throughout the world. A 2004 law passed by Congress officially designated the oak as America's national tree.

Most oaks are very variable in leaf size and shape. Smaller and larger leaves, leaves with shallow lobes and leaves with deeply indented lobes, and oddly shaped leaves may all be found even on a single tree. Leaves from the top of the tree which get a lot of sun ("sun leaves"), may differ from more shaded leaves from lower down on the same tree ("shade leaves"). Look at numerous leaves and use an "average" leaf as the basis for identification.

There are two major sub-groups of oaks: red oaks and white oaks.

RED OAK FAMILY

Bear Oak
Quercus ilicifolia
Look For: *A ground-hugging shrub or small tree, rarely more than 20 feet tall, growing in dry, well drained soils. Leaves may be shallow or moderately deeply lobed. Round acorn is striped above middle, has shallow cap (covering less than half the nut).*
Shape and Form: A shrub or small tree, usually less than 15' tall, with one or several twisted trunks and a rounded crown.

Distinguishing Between Red and White Oaks

Red Oaks	White Oaks
Lobes are usually pointed, with bristles at the tips. 	Lobes are usually rounded, with no bristles at the tips. 
Buds are relatively large, with bluntly or sharply pointed tips. 	Buds are relatively small, with blunt tips. 
Acorn caps are smooth; viewed with a hand lens, the inner surface of nut shells (not caps) is covered by fine hairs. Acorns require two years to mature, and both smaller one-year acorns and larger two-year acorns are found on the same tree. 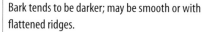	Acorn caps are knobby; the inner surface of nut shells (not caps) are smooth, not covered by fine hairs. Acorns take one year to mature; all acorns on a single tree are the same age class. 
Bark tends to be darker; may be smooth or with flattened ridges. 	Bark tends to be lighter (except for Chestnut Oak); blocky or flaky or scaly. 

Bark: Fairly smooth, gray to gray-brown, with a few raised lenticels. On older trees, becomes rough and scaly.

Leaves: Small leaves (3"–6") with 3–7 lobes, sometimes more blunt than pointed but still with a small bristle at tips and shallow or moderately deep sinuses. Glossy dark green above, lighter green or grayish green with fine silvery hairs underneath.

Acorn: Acorn ⅖"–⅘", pointed, nearly hemispherical, striped above middle. Shallow cap, covering ¼–½ nut.

Habitat: Well drained sandy or rocky soil, disturbed woodlands. Shade intolerant.

Wildlife Use: Bear Oaks provide the most important food source for 29 percent of endangered species of butterfly in Southern New England. The leaf litter is important for reptiles and amphibians.

Eastern Black Oak
Quercus velutina

Look For: *Rough bark, with flattish, whiteish ridges ("ski tracks") on upper trunk; lobed leaves with bristle-pointed tips to lobes and either shallow or deep sinuses separating the lobes. (Lower canopy leaves may be almost unlobed).*

Shape and Form: A medium-sized to large tree with a short, thick trunk, broad, rounded crown, and long horizontal branches near bottom.

Bark: Bark of young trees is dark gray and smooth (like that of Red Oak). Yellow or yellow-orange inner bark may show in furrows. Bark of mature trees is darker gray, with rough ridges broken by horizontal fissures into irregular rectangular blocks. The upper part of the trunk and branches may have flattish, whitish ridges that look like ski runs.

Leaves: Leaf shape is variable, but generally 5"–6" long, usually 5–7 lobed, with bristle-tipped points, and sinuses about halfway to midrib or less. Leaves are thicker, darker, and more glossy than red oak. Fine, yellowish-orange hairs may give edges and underside of

lower trunk

upper trunk with "ski tracks"

leaves a slightly orange hue. Shade leaves have much shallower sinuses and broader lobes. May retain its leaves in winter.

Buds: Buds are ovoid, about ¼"–½" long, somewhat hairy or fuzzy.

Acorn: Acorn is ovoid, up to ¾" long, often faintly striped. The shaggy, bowl-shaped, scaled cap covers ⅓– ½ of nut.

Habitat: Well drained soils.

Wildlife Use: Eastern Black Oak acorns are average in tannin and fat content. They are widely eaten by bears, deer, rodents, and wild turkeys. The trees form cavities easily and are a common site for cavity nesters.

Comment: Eastern Black Oak and Northern Red Oak are often hard to distinguish. They often hybridize, producing trees whose characteristics are intermediate between hose of the parent trees.

Pin Oak
Quercus palustris

Look For: *Lower branches droop downward; lobed leaves are deeply cut, with lower lobes angled nearly 90° to midline; tiny (less than ⅔") acorn.*

Shape and Form: A medium-sized to large tree with a large, pyramidal crown and conspicuously drooping lower branches.

Bark: Grayish-brown, with fine, shallow, vertical furrows. Reddish inner bark may show in furrows. In older trees, ridges become rougher and are broken,

especially at the base of the trunk, into squarish or irregularly rectangular blocks. May have small branchlets coming out of trunk and large limbs.

Leaves: Lobed leaves with very deep sinuses between 5–7 bristle-tipped lobes. The first and sometimes second lobe are at nearly 90° to axis. Top side is lustrous yellowish-green, with raised veins. Tufts of hair on underside where veins meet midvein. Often retains leaves through the winter.

Acorn: Tiny (less than ⅔" long), round to ovoid, vertically striped, with very thin, shallow, tightly scaled cap covering ¼ nut.

Habitat: Prefers wet areas along wetlands, streams, and ponds and grows in poorly drained soils, but can adapt to drier soils.

Comment: Lower limbs droop down, then turn up.

Wildlife Use: Pin Oak acorns are highly preferred by deer, squirrels, wild turkeys, and wood ducks. Their relatively small size makes them attractive to woodpeckers and other birds. Because Pin Oaks retain their leaves in winter, they provide valuable winter cover for songbirds and raptors.

Northern Red Oak

Quercus rubra

Look For: *Shallow lobed leaves with bristle-pointed tips to lobes and stems that are reddish at their base. (Leaves are thinner, often lighter, and less glossy than Eastern Black Oak). Dark brown bark, with flat, grayish ridges looking like "ski runs" on the trunk and branches. Large, somewhat elongated acorn with a shallow cap, covered by flat scales.*

Shape and Form: A medium to large tree, low branching, with a wide, rounded, low crown and stout, spreading branches.

Bark: Greenish-gray to dark gray, somewhat smooth in younger trees, with narrow vertical cracks showing light red inner bark and small, buff-colored lenticels. With age, becomes darker with dark furrows and lighter, long, vertical, parallel or flat-topped, loosely intersecting ridges, eventually becoming become broken into irregular vertical plates. Inner bark is brick brown. The ridges on the lower trunk are rough and uneven, but higher up remain smooth and whitish, looking like ski runs. The whitish stripes may extend down to 2 or 3 feet above ground level.

Leaves: 5"–8" long, smooth, duller and thinner than those of black oak, with 7–11 bristle tipped lobes. The sinuses dividing the lobes of leaves from the upper parts of the tree ("sun leaves") extend about halfway to the middle, and the leaves have reddish stems. The sinuses dividing the lobes of leaves from the lower parts of the tree ("shade leaves") are very shallow and the stems are sometimes reddish.

Buds: Buds are less than ⅓" long, pointed, smooth, and angular in cross section.

Acorn: 1"–1.5" long, round to ovoid. Cap is shallow, with flat scales, and usually covers only ¼ nut, but in some acorns may cover half of the nut.

Habitat: Grows best in moist, well drained soils.

Wildlife Use: Red Oak acorns are very high in protein, fat, and calories, but they are also more fibrous and tannic than acorns of other species of oak. They are not a preference of larger animals, but their persistence on the ground makes them an important food source for deer, bear, wild turkeys, and other animals. The leaves and twigs are eaten by deer, bear, porcupines, and flying squirrels.

Comment: Eastern Black Oak and Northern Red Oak are often hard to distinguish. They often hybridize, producing trees whose characteristics are intermediate between those of the parent trees.

Scarlet Oak
Quercus coccinea

Look For: *Deeply cut leaves with 5–7 lobes; bark with flat, whitish ridges looking like "ski runs" on upper trunk and branches. Acorns may have several rows of concentric rings at base and a thick, lumpy, bowl-shaped cap covering ⅓–½ the nut. Inner bark is pinkish red.*

Shape and Form: A medium-sized tree, with a rapidly tapering trunk, spreading branches, and a narrow, rounded crown.

Bark: Bark of young tree is fairly smooth, gray-brown, with narrow vertical cracks and areas of irregularly broken bark. Reddish inner bark is visible in cracks. Bark of older tree is dark gray/brown. The upper trunk has shallow furrows and flat, smooth ridges. Whitish ridges on upper part of trunk look like ski runs, ending 8–12 feet above the ground; below that the bark is blockier, with rough, irregular ridges, broken horizontally.

Leaves: Leaves are smaller (3"–6") than Red Oak. Five to seven deep lobes and sinuses. The leaves from the crown are very deeply lobed, with the divisions between lobes extending almost to the midrib. The leaves from the lower part of the tree have sinuses that extend about halfway to the middle, and the leaves have reddish stems. Tufts of hair on underside where veins meet midvein.

Acorn: Acorn ½" –1" long, round to ovoid, often with one or more rows of concentric rings at base. Bowl-shaped cap covers ⅓–½ nut.

Habitat: Adaptable. Prefers somewhat drier soils than red oak and on slopes tends to be more common than red oak on the upper part of the slope.

Wildlife Use: Similar to Black Oak. Scarlet Oaks retain their leaves through the winter so are an important source of winter cover.

lower trunk   upper trunk

	Distinguishing Among the Red Oaks				
	Bark	**Leaves**	**Terminal Buds/ Twigs**	**Acorns**	**Comments**
Bear Oak	Fairly smooth, gray to gray-brown, with a few raised lenticels. On older trees, becomes rough and scaly. Rarely exceeds 20 feet tall.	Small leaf (3"–6") with 3–7 lobes, sometimes more blunt than pointed, but still with small bristle at tips of lobes , and shallow or moderately deep sinuses. Glossy dark green above, lighter green or grayish green with fine silvery hairs underneath.	Reddish-brown, 1/8"–1/16" long, smooth with fine hairs, broadly conical with blunt tip.	Acorn 2/5"–4/5", pointed, nearly spherical, striped above middle. Shallow cap, covering 1/4–1/2 of the nut.	Well drained sandy or rocky soil. Shade intolerant.
Eatern Black Oak	Dark gray, with rough ridges broken by horizontal fissures into irregular rectangular blocks. May have flattish whitish ridges on upper trunk and limbs that look like "ski runs," or may have a more tire-tread like appearance. Inner bark is yellowish.	Leaf shape is variable, but usually 5–7 lobed, with bristle-tipped points and sinuses about halfway to midrib or less. Leaves are thicker, darker, and more glossy than red oak. Fine, yellowish-orange hairs on midvein may give edges and underside of leaves a slightly orange hue. Leaves from the lower part of the tree may have much shallower sinuses and broader lobes than those on upper part.	0.25"–0.5" long, gray or buff colored, very hairy or fuzzy; sharp-pointed. Twigs stout, drab brown, finely hairy or hairless	Up to 3/4" long, reddish-brown, ovoid, often faintly striped. The shaggy, bowl-shaped, scaled cap covers 1/3–1/2 of the nut.	Dry uplands and rich well-drained soil.

	Bark	Leaves	Terminal Buds/ Twigs	Acorns	Comments
Distinguishing Among the Red Oaks					
Pin Oak	Grayish-brown with fine, shallow, vertical furrows. May have small branches coming out of trunk and lower limbs. Lower branches droop, then turn up at ends.	5 to 7 bristle-tipped lobes, lustrous yellowish green, with raised veins, separated by very deep sinuses. The first and sometimes the second lobe are at nearly 90° to axis. Tufts of hair on underside where veins meet midvein.	Chestnut brown, round to ovoid, 0.08"–0.20" long, hairless except at tip, dully pointed. Twigs slender, reddish brown, hairless.	Less than ⅔" long, vertically striped, with a very thin, shallow, tightly scaled cap covering ¼ nut.	Prefers wet areas along wetlands, streams, and ponds but can adapt to drier soils.
Northern Red Oak	Dark gray. In younger tree, narrow vertical cracks with lighter inner bark showing through. In older trees, dark furrows and lighter, long, vertical, flat-topped, parallel, or intersecting ridges, broken into plates. Flat, whitened ridges often running to lower trunk look like ski runs."	7–11 bristle-tipped lobes, with sinuses extend about halfway to the middle for leaves from the upper parts of the tree, much shallower on leaves from the lower part of the tree. Leaves are smooth, duller and thinner than black oak and may have reddish stems. Underside is hairless except where side veins meet midvein.	Reddish-brown to very dark brown, round to ovoid, about 0.16"–0.3" long, mostly hairless but with frosty covering of hairs on margins. Twigs reddish brown, hairless	1"–1½" long. The cap is shallow, with flat scales, and usually (but not always) covers only ¼ of the nut.	Prefers rich, well drained soils.

Distinguishing Among the Red Oaks

	Bark	Leaves	Terminal Buds/ Twigs	Acorns	Comments
Scarlet Oak	Dark gray, with rough ridges broken by horizontal fissures into irregular rectangular blocks. Flattish, whitish ridges on upper and mid trunk and limbs look like "ski runs."	Five to seven lobes, bright green and shiny on top, smooth underneath. The leaves from the crown are very deeply lobed, with the divisions between lobes, set at an angle to the axis and extending almost to the midrib. Tufts of hair on underside where veins meet midvein. The leaves from the lower part of the tree have sinuses that extend about halfway to the middle. The leaves have reddish stems.	Reddish-brown, ⅛"–⅓" long, hairless or whitish and hairy near the dully-pointed tip. Twigs slender, reddish or orangish brown, hairless.	½"–1" long, round to ovoid. Often has several rows of concentric rings at base. The bowl-shaped cap covers ⅓–½ of the nut.	Adaptable. Prefers somewhat drier soils than red oak and may be more common than red oak on upper parts of slopes.

WHITE OAK FAMILY

Bur Oak (Burr Oak, Mossy Cup Oak)
Quercus macrocarpa
Look For: *"Fiddle-shaped" leaf, with irregular, rounded lobes, deeply indented near the middle, and a terminal lobe much larger than the other lobes. Bark has very deep furrows, and twigs have corky "wings." Acorn is very large (up to 2" diameter), elongated, more than half covered by cap, and the margins of the cap have a long fringe.*
Shape and Form: A medium-sized to large tree with a stout trunk, rounded, spreading crown, stout, low-spreading limbs, and corky wings on small branches.
Bark: Very rugged, pale gray bark, with long rectangular blocks at odd angles in a very "disorganized" or "chaotic" pattern. Newer branches may have corky "wings," which distinguishes it from Post Oak, whose leaves are similar.

branch with "wings"

Leaves: Large (6"–12"), shiny dark green on top, with 5–7 very deep, rounded, irregular lobes and a disproportionately large terminal lobe. The upper end of leaf is wider than lower part ("fiddle shaped") and the sinuses on lower part are much deeper than those at top. The sinus at midleaf is usually (but not always) especially deep, dividing the leaf into two distinct parts.

Acorn: Large (¾"–2" diameter), elongated, half or more enclosed by cap. The deep, thick, lumpy cap covers half or more of the nut. The margin of the cap is covered with a long fringe.

Habitat: Fairly adaptable; prefers sunny, moist, rich soils and poorly drained sites.

Wildlife Use: Despite their low tannin content, the large size of the acorns and the thickness of their cap restricts their use to larger animals such as deer and bear. Bur Oaks are especially attractive as nesting sites for songbirds.

Comments: Bur Oak is listed by the Connecticut Department of Energy and Environmental Protection (DEEP) as being "of special concern."

Chestnut Oak
Quercus prinus

Look For: *Unique, deeply furrowed bark forming longish, vertical blocks; elongated obovate leaves with many coarse, rounded teeth rather than fully formed lobes. Grows in dry, rocky, upland areas. Acorn is elongated, with a thin, saucer-shaped cap, with somewhat warty scales, covering ⅓ to ½ the nut.*

Shape and Form: A medium-sized to large tree with conspicuously rugged bark and a broad, open crown.

Bark: Reddish-brown to dark brown, smooth on young trees but in older trees *very* rugged, with deep, flat-topped vertical ridges and very deep furrows forming longish vertical blocks. Each block is about 4–5 times longer than wide.

Twigs: Stout; dark green to reddish brown; tips of buds are pointed.

Leaves: Elongated obovate, 4"–8" long, with many coarse rounded teeth. Top shiny yellowish-green, bottom may be slightly hairy along veins.

Acorn: Chestnut brown, 1"–1½" long, elongated, with a thin, saucer-shaped cap covering ⅓–½ the nut. Cap has somewhat warty scales.

Habitat: Most frequently found in dry, rocky upland areas.

Wildlife Use: Although the large size of the acorns makes them too large for most birds to eat, Chestnut Oak acorns are highly preferred by deer, squirrels, wild turkeys.

Comments: Chestnut oak is one of the most preferred host species for the gypsy moth, which defoliates trees.

Chinquapin Oak (Chinkapin)
Quercus muehlenbergii

Look For: *Small- to medium-sized tree with scaly bark, obovate leaves with coarse teeth, and a small acorn.*

Shape and Form: Usually a small- to medium-sized tree but can be large, with an irregular crown

Bark: Ashy gray with flaky, square scales separated by shallow fissures. The outer bark can be easily rubbed off. Brown to gray; tips of buds are blunt.

Twigs: Slender; brown to gray; tips of buds are blunt.

Leaves: Elliptical to obovate, pointed at the tip, usually with coarse teeth curved to point towards the leaf tip, each tooth ending in a small, round gland, best seen with a hand lens. The gland may make the leaf look like lobe tips are pointed, but there is no bristle. About 3"–6" long, widest just above the middle. Dark green above, paler and covered with tiny hairs underneath.

Acorn: Small (½"), ovoid, with a warty cap that covers almost half of the nut. Ripe fruit is very dark.

Habitat: Most common on dry banks of rivers and streams; occasionally in dry woods.

Wildlife Use: The relatively "sweet" acorns are heavily favored by songbirds, deer, small mammals.

Post Oak
Quercus stellata

Look For: *Obovate lobed leaves, deeply divided below middle lobe.*

Shape and Form: A small- to medium-sized tree with a stout, gnarled branches and a dense, rounded crown.

Bark: Light gray, fissured.

Leaf: 6"–10" long, narrower at base than towards tip, with 4–8 lobes. The two middle lobes are larger, squarish, with edges at nearly right angles to axis. The leaf is often deeply divided below these middle lobes, resulting in an overall appearance like a cross or violin. Upper surface is lustrous green, a bit rough-to-the-touch; lower surface is yellowish and covered with fine hairs. The leaves are similar to those of Bur Oak, but the latter has corky wings on the twigs.

Twig: Gray or yellowish, covered with a dense mat of hairs. Unlike Bur Oak, whose leaves are similar, branches are not winged.

Acorn: ⅖"–⅘" round to ovoid nut covered ⅓–½ by cap. Acorn is smaller than that of Bur Oak and lacks a fringe.

Habitat: Dry, rocky or sandy ridges and dry woodlands.

Wildlife Use: The acorns are used by wild turkeys and many mammals.

Branches and cavities in the trunk provide nesting sites for birds and small mammals.

Swamp White Oak
Quercus bicolor

Look For: *Obovate, deeply toothed leaves (about 5–7 "teeth" per side), extremely variable in shape, with a conspicuously silver-white, "felt-y" lower surface; peeling bark evident on small branches. Usually found in a moist habitat. Acorn is ⅓"–⅔" enclosed by a warty, slightly fringed cap, and often has a long stalk.*

Shape and Form: A medium-sized to large tree with a narrow, irregular crown and mix of ascending branches high up and drooping branches lower down.

Bark: Young trees have flaky, peeling bark with an orange inner bark. Bark of older trees is dark gray-brown with small blocky, flat, irregular ridges. Ridges are smaller (typically ½"–¾" wide, 1"–2" long), less pronounced than Chestnut Oak.

Twigs: Light brown; orange-brown buds have blunt tips.

Leaves: 4"–6" leaves, strikingly obovate with a triangular, dully pointed base and top half very shallowly lobed or coarsely toothed (5–10 teeth per side). Dark green above. Bottom surface is conspicuously silvery white and feels "felt-y."

Acorn: Light brown, 1" long, ⅓–⅔ enclosed with a warty, slightly fringed cap; often has a long stalk.

Habitat: Moist sites, wetland edges, poorly drained land.

Wildlife Use: Because Swamp White Oak grows in wetlands, its acorns are especially important for mallards and wood ducks.

Eastern White Oak
Quercus alba

Look For: *(Usually) 9 lobed leaves with rounded tips; grayish, platy bark sometimes looking like vertical shingles. Acorn is usually oblong, about 1" long, with about ¼ of nut covered by a cap with thick, warty scales.*

Shape and Form: A large tree with a short trunk, widely spreading branches, and a rounded crown, with some stout branches at nearly right angles to the trunk.

Bark: Mature bark is variable. Light to ashy gray, with moderately deep furrows and flat, vertical ridges broken horizontally, forming long peeling ridges or small, fairly regular elongated blocks or scales (typically ½"–1" wide by 2"–6" long). May be more blocklike at base of trunk, more shinglelike higher up.

Leaves: Leaves are highly variable in shape and size. Usually 9 rounded, smooth-edged lobes, each slightly divided in the middle, 4"–7" long, bright green on top, paler below. Dried leaves often remain on the tree in winter.

Acorn: ½"–1" long, light brown, usually oblong but varies, with about ¼ of nut covered by the cap, which has thick, warty scales.

Habitat: Most common in transition and upland forests, well drained soils, but fairly tolerant.

Wildlife Use: Most wildlife prefer the lower tannin acorns of White Oak to those from other oak species.

	Bark	Leaves	Terminal Buds	Acorn	Comments
Bur Oak	Rugged, grayish-brown, with long rectangular blocks in a disorganized pattern. Newer branches may have corky "wings."	"Fiddle-shaped": 5–7 very deep, rounded lobes, usually with an especially deep indentation mid-leaf.	⅛", round, gray, somewhat hairy.	Large (up to 2"), ovoid, half or more enclosed by cap. Margin of cap is covered by a long fringe.	A species "of special concern." Fairly adaptable, including poorly drained sites.
Chestut Oak	Reddish to dark grayish brown; very rugged with flat-topped ridges and very deep furrows forming longish rectangular blocks, each 4–5 times longer than wide.	Elongated, oval or obovate, with many coarse, rounded teeth. Top yellowish-green, bottom hairy.	Deep brown, ¼", conical.	1"–1.5" long, elongated, with a thin, saucer-shaped cap with somewhat warty scales covering ⅓ to ½ of the nut.	Most common in dry, rocky upland areas.
Chinquapin Oak	Ashy gray with flaky square scales separated by shallow fissures. The outer bark can be easily rubbed off.	Elliptical to obovate, pointed at the tip, usually with coarse, pointed teeth curved to point towards the leaf tip. Dark green above, paler and covered with tiny hairs underneath.	⅛", chestnut brown, ovoid or near-conical, hairless or almost so.	Small (½") nut. Warty cap covers almost half of the nut. Ripe fruit is very dark.	Most common on dry banks of rivers and streams; occasionally in dry woods.

Distinguishing Among the White Oaks

	Bark	Leaves	Terminal Buds	Acorn	Comments
Post Oak	Light gray, fissured.	Obovate, with 4–8 lobes. The two middle lobes are larger, with edges at nearly right angles to axis. The leaf is often deeply divided below these middle lobes. Upper surface is lustrous green, a bit rough-to-the-touch.	⅛", orange-brown, ovoid or near-conical, somewhat hairy.	⅖"–⅘" long, ovoid. Cap covers ⅓–½ of the nut.	Dry, rocky or sandy ridges and dry woodlands.
Swamp White Oak	Dark gray-brown with small blocky, flat, irregular ridges. Ridges are smaller (typically ½"–¾" wide, 1"–2" long), less pronounced than chestnut oak.	Leaves strikingly obovate with a triangular, dully pointed base and top half very shallowly lobed or coarsely toothed. Bottom surface is silvery white and feels "felt-y."	⅛", light brown, ellipsoid or nearly spherical, hairless save for whitish hairs near tip.	1" long. The warty, slightly fringed cap covers about ⅓–⅔ of the nut. Often has a long stalk.	Moist sites, wetland edges, poorly drained land.
White Oak	Light to ashy gray with moderately deep furrows and flat vertical ridges broken horizontally, forming long peeling ridges or small, fairly regular elongated scales.	Leaves variable. Usually 9 rounded, smooth-edged lobes, with each lobe often indented in the middle.	Deep brown, ⅛"–¼", ellipsoid or nearly spherical, hairless.	½"–1" long, usually oblong. Cap covers about ⅓ nut and has thick, warty scales.	Most common in well drained transition and upland forests, but adaptable.

COMMON PERSIMMON
Diospyros virginiana
Look For: *Bark divided into squarish blocks, resembling charcoal briquette; orange ripe fruit in Fall.*
Shape and Form: Small- to medium-sized tree with a narrow, rounded crown, crooked branches.

Bark: Dark gray-brown, divided into square, scaly, thick plates sometimes described as looking like charcoal briquettes.

Leaves: Oblong to oval, 2.5"– 5" long, with a rounded or wedge-shaped base and a short, pointed tip. Edges wavy but smooth.

Flowers: ½" long whitish or greenish-yellow flowers in late spring. Male trees have groups of 2 or 3 flowers, female trees solitary flowers.

Fruit: A large (1"–2" diameter), rounded, edible berry, turning yellowish to orange when ripe in late summer or early fall.
Habitat: Adaptable.
Wildlife Use: Leaves and twigs are browsed by deer. The fruit is eaten by deer, foxes, bears, rodents, and other mammals and by various birds.
Comment: The name "persimmon" is of Algonquin Indian origin. The genus name *Diospyros* is a Greek word meaning "fruit of the gods."

AMERICAN PLUM
Prunus Americana
Look For: *A shrub or small, shrubby tree, sometimes forming thickets.*
Shape and Form: A shrub or small, shrubby tree (usually less than 25' tall), often with multiple trunks and a broad, rounded crown and spiny branches. May form thickets.
Bark: In young trees, brown, smooth, with numerous horizontal lenticels, turning tan or gray or dark brown, scaly or with irregular ridges and peeling. Twigs may have thorns.
Leaves: 2"–4" long, ovate to elliptical, with a long, tapering point and finely singly or doubly toothed edges.

Flowers: White, about 1" diameter, singly or in clusters at the juncture between the stem and a leaf. Fragrant but with an unpleasant odor. Appear in early spring before the leaves.

Fruit: Red to yellow, almost spherical, about ¾"–1" diameter, edible.

Habitat: Moist soils, stream banks, open woods and edges of woods.

Wildlife Uses: The fruits are eaten by many birds.

EASTERN REDBUD (JUDAS TREE)
Cercis canadensis

Look For: *A small understory tree with a short trunk and rounded crown, heart-shaped leaves, showy pink flowers in spring before the leaves appear, and dangling seed pods in fall (persisting into winter).*

Shape and Form: A shrub or small understory tree, usually less than 30 feet with a short, trunk and low, spreading branches.

Bark: In young trees, grayish brown, smooth, with orange furrows. In older trees, gray to reddish-brown with scaly ridges.

Leaves: Heart-shaped, with short, pointed tip, 3"–5" long, with smooth edges. Emerging leaves may be a golden-green.

Flowers: Showy, pink to light purple, ½" long, growing profusely along the branches in small clusters. Appear in early spring, before the leaves.

Fruit: Flattened, dry, brown, 2"–4" flat pods, maturing in late summer and persisting into winter.

Habitat: Moist or dry woods

Wildlife Uses: Many birds eat the seeds. Deer browse the foliage. A source of nectar for honey.

Comments: According to legend, Judas Iscariot hanged himself on a Middle Eastern relative (*C. siliquastrium*) of our native Redbud. The tree, formerly a stately tree with white flowers, was ashamed of its role. From then on, it wouldn't grow big enough to be used for hanging and the flowers blushed pink with shame. More likely, the name "Judas Tree" derives from its prevalence in Judea; hence "the Judea's tree."

SASSAFRAS
Sassafras albidum

Look For: *A small- to medium-sized understory tree, with three kinds of leaves on the same tree: some football-shaped; some two-lobed like a mitten; and some three-lobed.*

Shape and Form: A small-sized to medium tree with an irregular and crooked trunk and branches, and a usually flat-topped crown. May grow in thickets and be shrublike.

Bark: Smooth and gray when young, becoming reddish brown and deeply furrowed, with broad, flat, ropelike, intersecting ridges. Ridges may be covered with a grayish "wash."

Leaves: Distinguished by presence of three kinds of leaves on the same tree: Some football-shaped, some two-lobed like a mitten; and some three-lobed. Margins smooth. Leaves and stems are intensely aromatic when broken or crushed.

Fruit: ⅓" long dark blue berry in a conspicuous, reddish-stalked cup in fall.

Habitat: Adaptable.

Wildlife Use: For most animals, sassafras is not an important food source, though it may be a major browse for deer in some areas. Sassafras fruits are eaten by many birds and small mammals.

Comments: The roots, bark, and leaves of sassafras have been widely used for teas and other drinks ("root beer") and for medicinal purposes. However, there is little evidence of its medical efficacy and in 1979, the US Food and Drug Administration banned the use of sassafras after research found that it contains carcinogenic substances. According to Blue Shield, "One cup of strong sassafras tea is reported to contain as much as 200 mg of safrole, an amount that is four times higher than the amount considered potentially hazardous to humans if consumed regularly."

DOWNY SERVICEBERRY (SHAD BUSH, SHAD BLOW, JUNEBERRY)
Amelanchier arborea

ALLEGHENY SERVICEBERRY (SMOOTH)
Amelanchier laevis

Look For: *A shrub or small tree (often with several trunks) and white flowers in early spring. Allegheny Serviceberry and Downy Serviceberry are very similar and sometimes considered to be the same species. The two hybridize readily.*

Shape and Form: A shrub or small tree (usually less than 25') with a narrow crown and usually several trunks.

Bark: Smooth, grayish, sometimes with subtle, vertical, greenish streaks when young; darker with narrow, shallow, blackened cracks and thin, scaly ridges when older.

Twigs: New growth on Allegheny Serviceberry is purplish; on Downy Serviceberry it is reddish-brown to gray.

Leaf: Finely toothed, thin, ovate or obovate, about 3" long, with a rounded or heart shaped base. The leaves of Allegheny Serviceberry are often reddish or bronzish when first unfolding (later dull green) and are largely hairless; those of Downy Serviceberry are not reddish and are hairy on both upper and lower surfaces, especially when young.

Flowers: White flowers appear before leaves in early spring.

Fruit: ⅕"–⅗" in diameter, roundish fruits, pink turning purplish, in late spring. (One common name for Serviceberry is "Juneberry")
Habitat: Moist well-drained slopes, stream banks, woods.
Wildlife Use: The fruits are an excellent late spring/summer food source for most fruit-eating mammals.

SUMACS
Genus Rhus

There are more than a dozen species of sumac in the US, and at least three of these can be found in Connecticut. Most common are **Smooth Sumac** (*R. glabra*), **Staghorn Sumac** (*R. typhina*), and **Winged Sumac** (or **Shining Sumac**, *R. copallinum*).

Most Sumacs are shrubs, but they occasionally take the form of small trees, often with multiple trunks and usually less than 15'–20' tall. Sumacs are common on roadsides and field edges.

Sumacs are easy to identify as a group by their large (12"–24") pinnately compound leaves, each with 11–31 narrow, pointed, 1.5"– 4" long leaflets. In Fall, they bear large (6" long) clusters of small reddish berries at their branch tips. The fruits persist into winter.

The several species are most easily distinguished from one another by their twigs. Smooth Sumac has *hairless* twigs. The twigs of Staghorn Sumac are densely covered with *fuzzy, brownish hairs*. Winged Sumac twigs are covered with *velvety, reddish-brown hair* and have *conspicuous wings*, up to ⅙" wide.

AMERICAN SYCAMORE (BUTTONWOOD TREE, BUTTONBALL TREE)
Platanus occidentalis
Look For: *Mottled, "camouflage"-like bark, especially on upper trunk and branches; large, 3–5 lobed leaves; dangling "buttonballs" in fall persisting into winter.*

Shape and Form: A massive tree with large, spreading branches and mottled bark peeling off in large pieces. In winter, the brown, one inch-diameter fruits remain on the tree.

Bark: Bark at base has steep, narrow furrows, broken horizontally into small blocks or scales (about ½" wide, 1"–1½" long); above that, pale green to white

   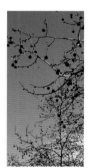

or mottled bark; creamy-white to greenish-white where bark has peeled away in large pieces. The peeling section may begin near the base of the tree or higher up on the trunk or may be seen only on the upper branches.

Leaves: Large (up to 9" wide and wider than long), with 3–5 lobes. Tips of lobes are short and pointed,

base of leaf is flat or deeply indented (heartlike), and edges are smooth or coarsely toothed.

Fruit: Brown 1" diameter heads of seeds ("buttonballs") dangling on long stems and persisting through most of winter.

Habitat: Moist rich soils, rich bottomlands, old pastures, edges of streams or wetlands.

Wildlife Use: The seeds (in the buttonballs) provide late winter food for finches, pine siskin, and juncos. Sycamores provide many cavities for cavity nesters. The leaf litter is especially valuable to earthworms.

TULIPTREE (YELLOW POPLAR, TULIP POPLAR)
Liriodendron tulipifera

Look For: *A large tree with a tall, branch-free trunk and a pyramidal crown of squarish, lobed leaves, yellow tulip-shaped flowers in spring, and tulip-shaped clusters of samaras remaining on tree in winter.*

Shape and Form: A large tree with a limb-free trunk and a pyramidal or oval crown.

Bark: The Tuliptree has a very tall, branch-free trunk. The bark of young trees has dark chevrons; bark of mature trees has deep fissures and interlacing ridges.

dried fruit

fruits on tree

Leaves: Distinctive, lobed leaf, about 5" long, with broad base and shallowly notched tip; edges smooth or a few teeth.

Flowers: Tulip-shaped yellow flowers, after leaves appear.

Fruit: A conelike structure, 2"–4" long, made up of multiple 2 seeded samaras, joined at base, and persisting into winter The samara clusters, like the flowers, are shaped something like a tulip.

Habitat: Transition forests.

Wildlife Use: Over-wintering purple finches eat the seeds on the trees. The pollen is a major and values source of honey.

BLACK TUPELO (SOUR GUM, BLACK GUM)
Nyssa sylvatica

Look For: *Narrow, elliptical, dark green leaves with a very straight trunk and branches spreading horizontally from the trunk like spokes on a wheel; blocky bark.*

Shape and Form: A medium-sized tree with a very straight trunk and branches at right angles to trunk, like spokes on a wheel, and a broadly conical or flat-topped crown.

Bark: The bark is grayish to brownish, deeply vertically furrowed, forming blocky rectangles.

Leaves: Oval to obovate, with a bluntly pointed tip, shiny, dark green, margins smooth or with a few large teeth, often clustered near the tips of branches.

Habitat: Moist, well drained sites in woods; along streams and wetlands.

Wildlife Use: The fruits are heavily used by robins, other thrushes, cedar waxwings, pleated woodpeckers, and other birds, while they are still on the tree.

Foxes, raccoons, and deer, wild turkeys, and grouse eat the fruit after it falls from the tree. An attractive nesting site for songbirds.

EASTERN WAHOO
Euonymus atropurpureus
Look For: *A shrub or occasionally a small tree, with oppositely arranged leaves, an irregular crown and striking, red or purple fruits in fall.*
Shape and Form: An upright, low branching shrub or small tree (up to 25') branching close to the ground to form an irregular crown.
Bark: Thin, brown with greenish-brown streaks. In larger, treelike Wahoos, the bark has distinctive, intricately intersecting light brown ridges and dark furrows.
Twigs: Green turning brown with age, sometimes 4-sided or slightly winged.
Leaves: Oppositely arranged, elliptical or ovate, 2"–4" long, finely toothed, with an abrupt long point.
Fruit: 4–lobed seed capsules, each ½" across, containing 1–2 seeds; green in mid-summer, turning red to purple in fall.
Habitat: Moist soils, thickets, forest edges
Wildlife uses: All parts of the plant are poisonous to humans, but the fruit are eaten by several species of bird.

BLACK WALNUT
Juglans nigra
Look For: *Long (up to 2 feet), alternate, pinnately compound leaves with elongated ovate leaflets; large (2') husked fruits.*
Shape and Form: A medium-sized to large tree with a rounded, open crown.
Bark: Light gray brown or reddish brown, (darker in older trees), rough, with irregular, interlaced ridges.
Leaves: Long (up to 24"), pinnately compound leaves, with 8–23 toothed, narrowly ovate or lanceolate leaflets, pointed tip. Often the leaflet at the tip is missing. End leaflets may be noticeably smaller than others.

Fruit: 2"–3" diameter green husked fruit.

Habitat: Well drained lowland woods and slopes.

Wildlife Use: Many animals, including raccoons, squirrels, wild turkeys, and bear eat the nuts. Black Walnuts secrete a toxic substance (*juglone*) that inhibits the growth of other plants under the tree.

Comment: The nuts of Black Walnut are difficult to extract from the thick shell but are edible for humans.

(Black Walnut and White Walnut, also called Butternut, are very similar. To distinguish between them, see p. 95.)

BLACK WILLOW
Salix nigra

Look For: *A small- to medium-sized tree with a short, often leaning trunk or multiple trunks and an irregular crown of very narrow, elongated leaves. Usually found in a wet area.*

Shape and Form: A small to medium-sized tree, with a trunk often dividing into two or more trunks near the ground and an irregular, rounded crown.

Bark: Thick, dark brown to nearly black, deeply furrowed with flat, scaly, interconnected ridges. May be shaggy.

Leaves: Narrowly lanceolate (up to 5" long), finely toothed, with long, tapering tip. Leaves are often curved towards tip.

Habitat: Typically grows along streams, wet depressions, and other wet areas.

Wildlife Use: Willows stabilize streambanks. Deer, beaver, muskrat, and porcupines eat the twigs, buds, leaves, and fruit. They are of especially high value to many insects, including butterflies and aphids.

Comment: *Salicin*, derived from the bark of willows, is an analgesic. In 1897 a modified form, acetylsalicylic acid, was marketed as the familiar Aspirin.

WHITE WILLOW
Salix alba
Look For: *A medium-sized tree, often with the trunk branching into sub-trunks close to the ground, drooping branch tips, and very long, slender leaves.*
Shape and Form: 1–4 trunks, open crown, drooping branches.
Bark: Brown, becoming furrowed.

Distinguishing Among the Willows		
	Black Willow	**White willow**
Shape	Single trunk, often leaning, or multiple trunks. Messy looking, with irregular clumps of twigs.	Short, stout trunk (sometimes split into 2 or 3 sub-trunks near ground). Broad, rounded crown with low, long pendulous branches.
Bark	Dark brown to black; deep fissures and interlacing, forking ridges, flaky/scaly.	Dull grayish to dull brownish; rough and coarsely ridged.
Twigs	Smooth, greenish to orangish-brown to dark brown (reddish to grayish in young twigs). Somewhat brittle at base.	Hairy, yellowish-brown to reddish-brown to brown (greenish-yellow in young twigs). Flexible.
Leaves	3"–6" long by 0.3"–0.7" wide, pointed, often slightly curved to one side ("sickle-shaped"). Shiny dark green above, pale green below.	2"–5" long by 0.3"–1.0" wide, pointed. Shiny dark green above (may have gray-green or bluish tint), pale whitish green and silky beneath.
Buds	2–4mm (0.8"–0.16") long. Reddish-brown.	1–3 mm (0.04"–0.12") long. Greenish-yellow.

Leaves: Narrowly lanceolate, 2"–4" long, finely toothed, with long, tapering tip. Leaves are straight. Underside of leaves is pale whitish green. One of first trees to leaf out in Spring.

Habitat: Typically grows along streams, wet depressions, other areas with a high-water table.

Comments: White Willow was introduced from Europe in colonial times. It has naturalized in Connecticut and is now more common than the "native" Black Willow. White and Black Willow frequently hybridize.

WINTERBERRY
Ilex verticillata

Look For: *Usually a shrub with multiple stems, but sometimes a small tree (usually less than 15', rarely to 25'), with ovate leaves and in fall and early winter, numerous, conspicuous red berries.*

Shape and Form: A tall shrub or small tree.

Bark: Gray, dark gray, or brown, smooth with conspicuous, warty lenticels

Leaves: Ovate, widest near middle, toothed, with conspicuous slender point at tip.

Flowers: White or greenish-white flowers in spring.

Fruit: Showy, bright red, round berries (on female plants only) lasting well into fall, long after leaves have fallen.

Habitat: Swamps, wet woods, stream margins.

Wildlife Use: The berries, mature in late fall, but they are relatively low in nutritious value. The unripe fruits also contain chemical compounds that protect them from attack by insects, fungi, and viruses, and protect them from damage from freezing, but that make them taste bad to birds. With repeated freezing and thawing, these chemicals gradually break down, but in the case of winterberry, relatively slowly compared to the fruits of other trees. The gain to the plant is presumably the benefits of avoiding the seasons of heaviest damage from microbes and insects. By mid-winter, when other food is less plentiful, the birds must eat what is available, and by then the Winterberry berries have become less unpalatable. It is common to see a Winterberry covered with fruit one day in mid or late winter and entirely denuded the next day.

Comments: Winterberries are dioecious (i.e., they have separate male and female plants). Only the female plants produce the red berries. Generally, one male winterberry can pollinate several female plants. When you see a female plant with berries, look for a male plant nearby.

WITCH HAZEL
Hamamelis virginiana
Look For: *A shrub or small tree (up to 25') with scalloped, often asymmetric leaves and yellow flowers in late fall/early winter.*

witch hazel leaf galls

Shape and Form: A shrub or occasionally a small tree (up to 20'–25' tall), with arching branches.

Bark: Gray, mottled with darker splotches.

Leaves: Darkish blueish green above, paler green below; ovate or obovate, with scalloped margins, often asymmetric base, and bluntly pointed tip. May have "witch hat"-shaped galls (green in summer, dark in fall) on upper surface of leaves.

Twigs: Twigs form zigzags, have conspicuous buds in winter.

Flowers: Yellow flowers in late fall/early winter.

Habitat: Moist slopes and woods; ravines.

Wildlife Use: The low branches of Witch Hazel provide nesting sites for wood thrushes and flycatchers. Nectar from the late-appearing flowers provides food for some insects in fall. "Y"-shaped twigs have been used as dowsing rods, supposedly showing the location of underground water.

Part III: Frequently Asked Questions

WHAT ARE THE MOST COMMON TREES IN CONNECTICUT?

Together, ten species comprise about three-quarters of the native forest trees in Connecticut. (https://ctpa.org/connecticuts-native-trees/). They are, with the estimated percent of trees each makes up:

- Red Maple—27 percent
- Black Birch—10 percent
- Eastern Hemlock—6 percent
- Sugar Maple—6 percent
- Northern Red Oak—6 percent
- American Beech—5 percent
- Eastern White Pine—4 percent
- Black Cherry—3 percent
- Yellow Birch—3 percent
- Pignut Hickory—3 percent

WHY DO TREES HAVE BARK?

Bark plays many roles in the life of a tree. It:

- Provides protection against fire
- Provides protection from insects, mammals, birds, fungi, epiphytes, parasites, bacteria
- Permits diffusion of oxygen and carbon dioxide into/out of the tree
- Retains water and facilitates adaptation to wet or dry conditions
- Provides protection against sun, heat, and rapid temperature change
- May engage in photosynthesis (e.g., birch, sycamore)
- Repairs damage/injuries

There are tradeoffs among these functions: For example, a thin bark that lets carbon dioxide and oxygen and water in and out is little protection against fire, and the converse. There are varying energy costs to having different forms of bark. Species that originally evolved in other climatic zones (e.g., the tropics) may still have characteristics reflecting their origin.

WHY DO TREES HAVE LEAVES?

The leaves are the site of "photosynthesis," the process in which plants combine carbon dioxide from the air, water from the soil, and energy from sunlight to make the sugars that provide the energy for all the other functions of the tree. Photosynthesis is carried out by sub-cellular structures called "chloroplasts," which are primarily found in the leaves. Water, in addition to being one of the ingredients used to make sugars, carries the sugars from the leaves where they are produced to the rest of the plant, and carries minerals from the soil to the leaves, bark, and growing shoot tips.

WHY DO BROADLEAF TREES LOSE THEIR LEAVES IN WINTER?

Most broadleaf trees shed their leaves all at once in the fall and winter. (Holly is an exception).

Trees must carry out a great balancing act:
- If a mature deciduous tree kept its leaves permanently, it wouldn't have to bear the cost of growing new ones each year (good). And the more leaf surface the tree exposes, the higher the rate of photosynthesis (also good). But the greater the leaf area, the higher the rate of water loss to the atmosphere (bad). And the greater the leaf area, the more the tree is subject to mechanical damage from high winter winds and heavy snow (more bad). The benefits of leaves to the tree are less in winter and the potential costs are greater.
- In the winter, there is less sunlight and freezing temperatures. Photosynthesis slows almost to a halt, but it still takes energy for the tree to run its leafy food factories and to transport water from the ground into the tree's trunk and leaves. It is more energy efficient for a leafy tree to close operations in the winter and go dormant.
- The leaves of deciduous trees are not protected against freezing. (The roots, branches, and twigs can endure freezing temperature.) Sometimes it warms up for a brief period in the middle of winter. If the tree had leaves, they would start photosynthesizing again. When the cold returns, the leaves would be caught with water in their veins and freeze and die. Then the tree would be left without leaves when spring finally returns.
- Leaves accumulate damage from insects over the course of the year. It may be less costly to lose the leaves once a year and re-grow them than to keep continuously repairing damaged leaves.
- Some species of deciduous tree flower early in the spring when they are still leafless. The absence of leaves improves wind transmission of pollen for wind-pollinated species such as maples and oaks and birches, and it increases the visibility of the flowers to insects in insect-pollinated trees such as Apple, Basswood, Black Locust, and Willow. So not having leaves in early spring increases the effectiveness of pollination.

Bottom line: In winter, the risks of holding on to the leaves outweigh the benefits. In fall, as winter approaches, the tree gets rid of them.

WHY DON'T CONIFERS LOSE THEIR LEAVES IN WINTER?

Most conifers are "evergreen." That is, they stay green all year long. (Tamarack, which loses its needles each fall, is an exception). But in fact, conifers do shed their needles, just not all at once in the fall. Rather they shed a fraction of their leaves each year, spread out from summer through fall. Depending on the species, they lose anywhere from one-half to perhaps one-seventh of their needles each year.

This is a strategy that works for trees that live in colder, dryer climates. The thin, narrow needles have less surface area exposed to the air and lose less water than the broader leaves of deciduous trees. Their shape (as well as the conical shape of most conifers) also makes it harder for snow to accumulate on them, so the tree is less weighed down and damaged by snow. Thus, retaining leaves in the winter does not pose the problems for conifers to the same degree as for broad leaf trees. Conifers may not carry out much photosynthesis during the colder, darker months of winter, but when spring comes, they are ready to start producing sugars. And they do not need to devote energy to producing a whole new set of leaves each year.

WHY DO SOME BROADLEAF TREES HOLD ON TO THEIR DEAD LEAVES IN WINTER?

Some broadleaf trees retain their *dried* leaves in winter. This is called "marcescence." Marcescence is common among many oak species, beech, witch hazel, hornbeam, and hophornbeam trees. It appears especially on younger and smaller trees and on branches nearer the ground.

No one knows exactly why this occurs. Some scientists speculate that retaining some of the leaves may help deter deer and other browsers from nibbling on the twigs and buds. Retained leaves may also help protect the twigs of the young trees from exposure to damaging winds. And a number of scientists have suggested that young understory trees, especially those on marginal soil, may hold on to their leaves, releasing them only in early spring, just in time for the nutrients from the old leaves to be available for spring growth.

WHY DO LEAVES COME IN DIFFERENT SIZES AND SHAPES?

If leaves make it possible for trees to produce their own food, why hasn't evolution lead to all trees having a leaf that has the optimal shape for photosynthesis? There is no clear answer to this, but there are several theories. The starting point is that there are multiple demands on leaves and that these different demands require different sizes and shapes.

Leaves carry out photosynthesis (which means they must intercept light and absorb energy from the sun); take up water and materials dissolved in water from the roots; export sugars made in the leaf to the rest of the tree; and exchange gases with the atmosphere. But they also must dissipate heat, cope with wind and other externally applied mechanical forces; cope with insets, mammals, fungi, and other organisms that try to eat them; and enable the penetration of light to the inner portions of the tree.

Various characteristics of leaves have an impact on the leaves' ability not only to carry out photosynthesis, but to meet these other obligations, as well. For example:

- Larger leaves carry out more photosynthesis (like a larger solar panel on the roof of a building), but smaller leaves are less prone to damage from harsh conditions (cold, heat, dryness, etc.).
- The rate of heat transfer across a lobed leaf is greater than that of an unlobed leaf of the same area.
- Lobed leaves carry water more efficiently from the stem to the rest of the leaf.
- Toothed leaves lose more water than leaves without teeth. At the beginning of the growing season, this pulls more water up from the roots and may "jumpstart" the photosynthetic season.
- In general, trees that tolerate shade have thinner, larger leaves oriented horizontally, horizontal branches, larger seeds, and a relatively large crown. Trees that are less shade tolerant have thicker, smaller, more erect leaves, erect branches, smaller seeds, and a relatively small crown.
- Leaves at the top of a tree get more sun; leaves at the bottom are more in the shade. Shade leaves have a larger area and are less lobed so as to catch more light; are darker green (they contain more chlorophyll); and tend to be thinner so that the chloroplasts on the upper surface don't shade out those at the bottom. Sun

leaves are thicker to protect the chloroplasts against destruction of their chlorophyll by too much sunlight.

- The needles of evergreen trees, due to their thinner and narrower shape as well as the waxy coating that many evergreen needles have, lose less water than the flat, wide leaves of deciduous trees. The needles also have lower wind resistance than broad leaves. It's difficult for snow to remain on the narrow needles, so the tree is less weighed down by snow. Evergreens do shed their needles, but only gradually and not all at once. As a result, the tree can devote less energy to growing a complete set of new leaves each year.

Depending on where the tree evolved and the conditions under which it evolved, there may be greater advantages or disadvantages to various combinations of leaf size, shape, and structure.

WHY ARE SOME TREES FOUND ONLY IN CERTAIN AREAS?

Different species of trees tend to grow in different habitats. Some prefer wetter sites, others drier; some sunnier sites, others shadier. Some want acidic soil, others "sweet" (alkaline) soil. In some cases, the tree *only* grows in a certain kind of habitat. In others the tree *prefers* certain habitats but will sometimes grow in other areas. And some trees are *adaptable*, growing in a wide variety of habitats equally well.

Note that some trees may appear on more than one of the following lists. Shade tolerance is indicated as T (tolerant), M (moderately tolerant), or I (intolerant)

Trees that grow in wetlands or on land that is sometimes covered with water or sodden:
- Green Ash (T)
- Yellow Birch (M)
- Cottonwood (I)
- Dogwood (T)
- Black Maple (M)
- Swamp White Maple (M)
- Red Maple (T)
- Pin Oak (I)
- Sycamore (I/M)
- Tulip Tree (I)
- Black Tupelo (I)
- Black Willow (I)

Trees that prefer moist but well drained sites:
- White Ash (M)
- Green Ash
- Quaking Aspen (I)
- Big Tooth Aspen (I)
- Basswood (M)
- Beech (T)
- Black Cherry (I)
- Paper Birch (I)
- Black Birch (M)
- Gray Birch (I)
- Yellow Birch (M)
- Chestnut (M)
- Dogwood (T)
- American Elm (M)
- Bitternut Hickory (M)
- Pignut Hickory (M)
- Shagbark Hickory (M)
- Hophornbeam(T)
- Ironwood (T)
- Black Locust (M)
- Black Maple (M)
- Red Maple (M)
- Striped Maple (T)
- Sugar Maple (T)
- Black Oak (M)
- Bur Oak (M)
- Pin Oak (I)
- Red Oak (M)
- Scarlet Oak (I)
- Swamp White Oak (M)
- White Oak (M)
- Sassafras (I)
- Tulip Tree (I)
- Black Tupelo (T)
- Black Walnut (I)
- Witch Hazel (T)

Trees that tend to grow on slopes or on dry, upland sites:
- Quaking Aspen (I)
- Big Tooth Aspen (I)
- Paper Birch (I)
- Black Birch (M)
- Gray Birch (I)
- Pignut Hickory (M)
- Black Oak (M)
- Bur Oak (M)
- Chestnut (M)
- Chestnut Oak (I)
- Scarlet Oak (I)

Trees that grow in areas that have been "disturbed" by fire, storm blowdown, or farming in an earlier era:
- Quaking Aspen (I)
- Gray Birch (I)
- Black Cherry (I)
- Black Locust (T)
- Tulip Tree (I)

CAN YOU TELL HOW OLD A TREE IS WITHOUT CUTTING IT DOWN?

You can estimate a tree's age (very roughly) by using a simple technique.

1. Determine the tree's diameter (inches) at a height of 4.5 feet from the ground. Or determine its circumference and divide by 3.14 to get the diameter.

2. Multiply the diameter (in inches) by the appropriate growth factor below to get approximate age. Calculators for estimating the age of other species can be found at http://www.tree-guide.com/tree-age-calculator and https://brockleytree.com/how-to-know-the-age-of-a-tree/.

Example: A beech tree has a circumference of 60 inches at 4.5 feet from the ground. Diameter = 60 ÷ 3.14 = 19 inches (approximately). 19 x 6 = 114 years (estimated age).

This method provides only a very crude estimate. The rate at which any particular tree grows is affected by genetic differences, the age of the tree, the altitude and other local site and climatic conditions, competition from other trees, the availability of water availability, the availability of nutrients in the soil, the presence of insects or diseases, and the general tree health.

Estimating the Age of a Tree	
Species	**Growth Factor**
Ash, White	5
American Beech	6
American Elm	4
Basswood	3
Paper Birch	5
Black Cherry	5
Black Locust	3.5
Cottonwood	2
Dogwood	7
American Elm	4
Shagbark Hickory	7.5
Horse Chestnut	8
Sugar Maple	5.5
Red Maple	4.5
White Oak	5
Northern Red Oak	4
Red Pine	5.5
White Pine	5
Hornbeam	7
Sycamore	4
Tuliptree	5
Black Walnut	4.5

These two white ashes were cut down at the same time. From counting the rings, we know that the tree on the left was 63 years old, the tree on the right was 86 years old. The guide above would suggest that the left-hand tree (13" diameter) was about 65 years old (very close), the right-hand tree (39" diameter) 195 years old (way off). The growth rings on the larger stump show that it grew very rapidly in its early years. By the age of 22 it was already as big as the smaller tree, though the chart would have suggested it was much older). Then its growth slowed down. By the time the left-hand tree had sprouted, the right-hand tree was already almost three feet in diameter. It presumably shaded out the younger tree, which grew less rapidly.

DO TREES INTERACT WITH ONE ANOTHER?

In natural habitats such as a forest, trees interact with a wide variety of organisms, including with other trees. These interactions enhance the evolutionary fitness of the trees and are the results of natural selection.

Some popular writers and even a few scientists have described these interactions as "communication" or even as a form of "consciousness," as if the trees "decide" to warn their neighbors about threats. But to say that trees have "consciousness" or to see these interactions as the result of a tree's "will" or "intentions" is anthropomorphic. Trees do not *choose* or *plan* their actions. Forest trees have evolved to thrive in interdependent communities and use each other to solve problems. But as a group of eminent scientists wrote recently, "There is no evidence that plants require [or] have evolved . . . mental faculties, such as consciousness, feelings, and intentionality, to survive or to reproduce."

Trees in a stable forest are connected to each other through underground networks of "mycorrhizal" fungi. The fungi produce branching filaments that surround the fine roots of the tree or even squeeze in between the cell walls and cell membranes of the root cells. The fungi and the trees have a symbiotic relationship. The fungi in effect extend the tree's root system, helping the tree absorb more water and minerals from the soil. The tree, in return, provides the fungi with as much as 30 percent of the sugar that it produces from photosynthesis.

Trees also interact through the air. When an herbivore such as a deer starts chewing on the tree's leaves, the tree detects the deer's saliva and produces substances that make the leaves taste bad. Some of the chemicals it produces for its own protection may be transmitted through the air to neighboring trees. The latter then also start producing the noxious chemicals. Similarly, when willows and sugar maples are attacked by insect pests, both they and neighboring trees pump out chemicals to repel the insects. Even more dramatically, when elms and pines come under attack from leaf-eating caterpillars, they detect the caterpillar's saliva and release pheromones that attract parasitic wasps. The wasps lay their eggs inside the caterpillars and the wasp larvae, when they hatch, eat the caterpillar from the inside out.

Trees may also share nutrients with other trees, using the mycorrhizal network. One study found that labelled carbon dioxide, absorbed by the leaves of a spruce tree, makes its way to the roots of neighboring trees, including trees of other species such as beech and pine. Other studies have shown that when a neighbor tree is struggling, other trees may detect their distress and increase the flow of nutrients. There is nothing "altruistic" about this. If a neighbor tree dies, it opens a gap in the tree canopy. Damaging winds can penetrate the forest more easily, and sunshine, reaching the forest floor, may weaken the mycorrhizae and dry out the evenly regulated microclimate that forest trees prefer.

Trees and other plants evolved along a very different pathway from animals. Animals get their food by preying on other animals and eating plants. They had to evolve to both find prey and escape themselves becoming prey, as well as to find mates. Bilateral symmetry, with a brain at one end of the body, enhanced mobility. Neurons and eventually, the brain—the underlying physical basis for consciousness, feelings, and intentionality—evolved to coordinate their efforts and enhanced their evolutionary fitness.

By contrast, plants get their mineral nutrients and water from the soil, their carbon from the air, and their energy from the sun. They evolved to compete for sunlight and soil resources, not to chase prey or evade predators. In flowering plants, co-evolution with insects and other animals created the "mobility" needed for cross-pollination, obviating the need to themselves develop these traits. As a result, they do not require, and thus did not evolve, energy-expensive mental faculties such as consciousness or feelings to survive or reproduce.

WHAT ARE THE THINGS I SEE ON THE OUTSIDE OF TREES THAT ARE NOT BARK?

Burl (an abnormal tree growth, usually caused by an injury or an infection)

Marks from a bear's claws

Damage from the Emerald Ash Borer

"Target canker" on Red Maple

Holes made by a Yellow Bellied Sapsucker

Holes made by a Pileated Woodpecker

IS THERE SUCH A THING AS A "WOLF TREE"?

Most of the trees in the woods are tall and narrow, their lowest branches high up on the trunk. As a result, their leaves are exposed to the sun and not shaded out by other neighboring trees. But a few trees may look like the trees in a child's picture book, with widely spreading branches starting relatively low on the trunk.

Seventy-five and more years ago, when farmers cleared the land for pasture, they often left a few trees standing on purpose (e.g., to provide shade for their animals) or accidentally. These trees, not competing with other trees, were able to spread their limbs wide. Later, when the fields were abandoned, other trees could not flourish under their deep shade, and the pasture tree survived.

Such trees suppress the reproduction of other trees in a circle around them with a radius of about 1 foot for each inch of the diameter of the trunk (a bit less for ash and basswood, a bit more for beech).

These are sometimes called "wolf trees" because they were seen by foresters as predators, taking sunlight and nutrients from the other straighter (and more economically valuable) trees around them. As ecologist Tom Wessels notes, like a lone wolf, they stand alone.

SOURCES AND RESOURCES

The descriptions of trees in this Field Guide were compiled from the descriptions in the following sources, verified and elaborated upon by my own observations.

Austin Hayes and Wilbur Mattoon, *Forest Trees of Connecticut* (orig. 1929; revised 2012, Connecticut Forest and Park Association).

Elbert L. Little, *The Audubon Society Field Guide to North American Trees* (Knopf, 1980).

Gil Nelson, Christopher J. Earle, and Richard Spellenberg, *Trees of Eastern North America* (Princeton University Press, 2014).

George A. Petrides and Janet Wehr, *Eastern Trees* (Peterson Field Guides; Houghton Mifflin, 1998).

David Allen Sibley, *The Sibley Guide to Trees* (Knopf, 2009).

George W.D. Symonds, *The Tree Book* (Quill/William Morrow, 1958).

Sally Weeks, Harmon P. Weeks, Jr., and George R. Parker, *Native Trees of the Midwest* (Purdue University Press, 2010).

Michael Wojtech, *Bark: A Field Guide to Trees of the Northeast* (University Press of New England, 2011).

The following websites also provided rich sources of information about the trees described in this guide:

US Government Websites

- Silvics of North America, https://www.srs.fs.usda.gov/pubs/misc/ag_654/table_of_contents.htm
- About Plants, https://plants.usda.gov/home
- Fire Effects Information System (US Department of Agriculture), https://www.feis-crs.org/feis/faces/SearchByOther.xhtml;jsessionid=DCDFECAADD8BBC41AAC30E0D329F0909

Other Websites

- Virginia Tech Dendrology, http://dendro.cnre.vt.edu/dendrology/
- Flora of North America, http://www.efloras.org/flora_page.aspx?flora_id=1
- Plant Database (Lady Bird Johnson Wildflower Center), https://www.wildflower.org/plants/result.php?id_plant=QUAL
- Connecticut Native Trees (Trees for Me), http://www.treesforme.com/ct_a-z.html

- What Tree is That? (Arborday Foundation) https://www.arborday.org/trees/whattree
- Common Ohio Trees, https://ohiodnr.gov/wps/portal/gov/odnr/discover-and-learn/plants-trees/common-trees-ohio/common-trees-ohio
- Environmental Horticulture (U. of Florida), https://hort.ifas.ufl.edu/database/trees/trees_common.shtml
- Go Botany (Native PlantTrust), https://gobotany.nativeplanttrust.org/dkey/#c3

PHOTO CREDITS

Save as noted below, photos are by John Ehrenreich and Diane Nizlek. All others are reprinted under Creative Commons licenses. Some of these have been cropped or rotated.

Abbreviations

CC BY-SA 3.0: Creative Commons Attribution ShareAlike Unported license
CC BY 2.0: Creative Commons Attribution 2.0 Generic license
CC BY-SA: Creative Commons Attribution Sharealike license
CC BY 3.0 US: Creative Commons Attribution 3.0 license
CC BY-ND 2.0: Creative Commons Attribution-NoDerivs 2.0 Generic license
CC BY-SA 4.0: Creative Commons Attribution-ShareAlike 4.0 International license

Page	Description	Credits and Sources
46	Black cherry flower:	rockerBOO / CC BY-SA 2.0. "02291 Black Cherry Flowers." https://ccsearch. creativecommons.org/photos/2cbbf262-d18a-4dad-9b85-9d26c2d44d6a
46	Basswood flowers:	Fritzflohrreynolds/ CC BY SA 3.0. File:Tilia americana - American Basswood.jpg. https://commons.wikimedia.org/wiki/File:Tilia_americana_-_American_Basswood.jpg
46	Catalpa flowers:	crudmucosa, CC BY 2.0. "Ruffled Catalpa Flowers." https://search.creativecommons.org/photos/1d7b124a-7847-4095-a803-4e31f6fbe4ce
47	Hawthorn flowers:	Kristine Paulus/CC BY 2.0. "File: Crataegus viridis 'Winter King,'" New York Botanical Gasrden.jpg. https://ccsearch.creativecommons.org/photos/92a61d3c-053d-4851-ab47-81167ed7ea10.

Page	Description	Credits and Sources
53	Nannyberry fruits:	Wendell Smith/ CC BY 2.0. "a cluster of nannyberries." https://ccsearch.creativecommons.org/ photos/50b59fc8-1efb-447a-b3c7-c3bbb9f5c810
52	Redbud seed pods:	Lambique,/ CC BY-SA 3.0. File:Redbud tree (Cercis canadensis) Close Up View.jpg, https://commons.wikimedia.org/wiki/ File:Redbud_tree_(Cercis_canadensis)_ Close_Up_View.jpg
53	Black Tupelo berries:	Dogtooth77/ CC BY-NC-SA 2.0. "Nyssa sylvatica fruit." https://ccsearch. creativecommons.org/photos/3e8b1eee-2027-4068-baab-8446949a0822
54	Sycamore buttonball:	Rasbak/CC BY-SA 3.0, File:Platanus occidentalis fruits.jpg. https://commons. wikimedia.org/wiki/File:Platanus_ occidentalis_fruits.jpg
54	Eastern Wahoo fruits:	Masebrock, English Wikipedia/public domain. File: Euonymus atropurpureus fruit. jpg. https://commons.wikimedia.org/wiki/ File:Euonymus_atropurpureus_fruit.jpg
53	Black Cherry fruit:	Frank Vincentz/CC BY-SA 3.0. File:Surwold - Neubörgerstraße - Sandberg + Prunus serotina 07 ies.jpg. https://commons. wikimedia.org/w/index.php?curid=75863308.
55	Red Maple bud:	Shaun C. Williams/CC BY 2.0. "Red Maple buds in winter." https://ccsearch. creativecommons.org/photos/c7694d36-ab18-4182-876a-d5cd065ef498

Page	Description	Credits and Sources
98	Pin Cherry bark:	Bill Cook, Michigan State University, Bugwood.org / CC BY 3.0 US. "Image number 1219173. pin cherry (Prunus pensylvanica)." https://www.forestryimages.org/browse/detail.cfm?imgnum=1219173
98	Pin Cherry leaves:	Rob Routledge, Sault College, Bugwood.org/ CC BY-SA 3.0." Image Number: 5461506, Pin Cherry Prunus pensylvanica. https://www.forestryimages.org/browse/detail.cfm?imgnum=5461506#collapseseven
115	Mountain Maple leaves:	Keith Kanotti, Maine Forest Service, Bugwood.org/CC BY 3.0. File:Acer spicatum 5349056.jpg. https://commons.wikimedia.org/wiki/File:Acer_spicatum_5349056.jpg
123	Mountain Ash bark:	Keith Kanoti, Maine Forest Service, Bugwood.org/ CC BY 3.0 US. Image Number 5349069 American Mountain Ash (Sorbus americana). https://www.forestryimages.org/browse/detail.cfm?imgnum=5349069
123	Mountain Ash leaves:	Keith Kanoti, Maine Forest Service, Bugwood.org/CC BY-SA 3.0. Image Number 530035 American mountain ash (Sorbus americana). https://www.forestryimages.org/browse/detail.cfm?imgnum=5350035
123	Mountain Ash berries:	Superior National Forest/ CC BY 2.0. File:Sorbus americana 4-eheep (5098078576).jpg, https://commons.wikimedia.org/wiki/File:Sorbus_americana_4-eheep_(5098078576).jpg

Page	Description	Credits and Sources
145	American Plum bark:	Matt Levin/CC BY SA 2.0. "Prunus Americana." https://ccsearch.creativecommons.org/photos/615bc270-248e-40d2-8050-f16dafb85c82
54	American Plum fruit:	Whitney Cranshaw, Colorado State University, Bugwood.org/ CC BY-SA 3.0. Image Number 5561489 American plum (Prunus americana). https://www.forestryimages.org/browse/detail.cfm?imgnum=5561489
145	Eastern Redbud bark:	Raul654/CC BY-SA 3.0 File: Cercis canadensis.jpg, https://commons.wikimedia.org/wiki/File:Cercis_canadensis.jpg
145	Eastern Redbud seed pod:	Lambique,/ CC BY-SA 3.0. File: Redbud tree (Cercis canadensis) Close Up View.jpg, https://commons.wikimedia.org/wiki/File:Redbud_tree_(Cercis_canadensis)_Close_Up_View.jpg

INDEX

ABOUT THE AUTHOR

John Ehrenreich has PhDs in biological sciences and in psychology. He is a volunteer at Connecticut Audubon's Deer Pond Farm sanctuary, where he co-leads nature walks and prepares educational materials. In his professional life he is a psychologist and a former professor of psychology at SUNY Old Westbury. He is the author or co-author of six other books, including *The American Health Empire* (Random House), *The Altruistic Imagination* (Cornell), and *Third Wave Capitalism* (ILR/Cornell). His articles have appeared in, among other places, *The Nation*, *Slate*, *American Prospect*, *Salon*, and *Washington Monthly*. He resides in Sherman, Connecticut.